D0880660

Prayer Book for
Young Catholics

Father Robert J. Fox

Prayer Book for Young Catholics

Our Sunday Visitor Publishing Division
Our Sunday Visitor, Inc.
Huntington, Indiana 46750

Nihil Obstat: Rev. Michael Heintz
Censor Librorum

Imprimatur: ✠ John M. D'Arcy
Bishop of Fort Wayne-South Bend
June 8, 2004

The *nihil obstat* and *imprimatur* are declarations that a work is free from doctrinal or moral error. It is not implied that those who have granted the *nihil obstat* and *imprimatur* agree with the contents, opinions, or statements expressed.

The Scripture citations used in this work have been adapted from *The Jerusalem Bible*, copyright © 1966 by Darton, Longman & Todd, Ltd., and Doubleday, a division of Random House, Inc. Reprinted by permission. All rights reserved.

Every reasonable effort has been made to determine copyright holders of excerpted materials and to secure permissions as needed. If any copyrighted materials have been inadvertently used in this work without proper credit being given in one form or another, please notify Our Sunday Visitor in writing so that future printings of this work may be corrected accordingly.

Copyright © 1977, 1981, 2004 by Our Sunday Visitor Publishing Division, Our Sunday Visitor, Inc.
14 13 12   5 6 7 8 9

All rights reserved. With the exception of short excerpts for critical reviews, no part of this work may be reproduced or transmitted in any form or by any means whatsoever without permission in writing from the publisher.
Write:

Our Sunday Visitor Publishing Division
Our Sunday Visitor, Inc.
200 Noll Plaza
Huntington, IN 46750

ISBN: 1-59276-098-8 (Inventory No. T150)
LCCN: 2004106545

Cover design by Tyler Ottinger
The Rosary illustration on page 164 has been provided by Our Sunday Visitor. All other interior illustrations have been provided by Father Robert J. Fox.
Interior design by Sherri L. Hoffman

PRINTED IN THE UNITED STATES OF AMERICA

Dedication

*To the Sacred Heart of Jesus and
to the Immaculate Heart of Mary.*

*To Blessed Jacinta, Blessed Francisco, and
Sister Lucia, the Fátima seers, who inspired many
of the prayers in this book.*

*To those who will use this book, of whom
I beg remembrance in their prayers.*

MARY, MOTHER OF GOD, by Basil Lynch

Our prayers should express our faith. Our faith should show in the way we pray. Therefore, if you pray these prayers from your heart, you will discover that you are learning the content of our holy Catholic faith at the same time.

Some of these prayers may prove to be favorites. You will then want to pray them more often. But, at other times, you should go aside in greater silence and pray those prayers less often used. In that way, you will advance in holiness. Your vision and concern for others, and for God Himself, will grow stronger.

What is needed is a *living* faith. Our faith must become alive in the ordinary events of daily living. The use of this prayer book will help you to make your entire life a prayer. It was Jesus who said that we should "pray always."

It is my belief that Our Lady was a catechist at Fátima, Lourdes, and at other times and places. Our Lady has taught children how to grow in holiness. Even children can offer simple prayers that are profound. I pray that this prayer book will be an invaluable aid in that direction.

FATHER ROBERT J. FOX

TABLE OF CONTENTS

II. BASICS OF THE FAITH

"What were you arguing about on the road?" [Jesus asked.] They said nothing because they had been arguing which of them was the greatest. So He sat down, called the Twelve to Him and said, "If anyone wants to be first, he must make himself last of all and servant of all." He then took a little child, set him in front of them, put His arms round him, and said to them, "Anyone who welcomes one of these little children in My name, welcomes Me; and anyone who welcomes Me welcomes not Me but the One who sent Me."

MARK 9:33-37

THE CHILD JESUS

Here is a ten-point program by which one may keep close to God:

- **Sign of the Cross:** first act of each day.
- **Morning prayers:** including the Morning Offering (page 26).
- *Angelus*: at noon and about 6:00 p.m. (page 35).
- **Aspirations:** short prayers during the course of the day.
- **Sacrifice of the Mass:** with reception of Holy Communion; regular reception of the Sacrament of Reconciliation (Penance).
- **Rosary:** daily, preferably with family members.
- **Visit to Jesus in the Blessed Sacrament:** once a week.
- **Spiritual reading and study:** about fifteen minutes a day.
- **Evening prayers:** including an examination of conscience.
- **Lay apostolate:** practical works, such as good example, to bring others to Jesus.

I
PRAYERS

Sign of the Cross

In the Name of the Father, and of the Son, and of the Holy Spirit. Amen.

Lord's Prayer
(Also called the Our Father)

Our Father, who art in heaven, hallowed be Thy name. Thy kingdom come, Thy will be done on earth as it is in heaven. Give us this day our daily bread; and forgive us our trespasses as we forgive those who trespass against us, and lead us not into temptation, but deliver us from evil. Amen.

Apostles' Creed

I believe in God the Father almighty, Creator of heaven and earth; and in Jesus Christ, His only Son, Our Lord; who was conceived by the Holy Spirit, born of the Virgin Mary; suffered under Pontius Pilate, was crucified, died, and was buried; He descended into hell; the third day He arose again from the dead; He ascended into heaven, and is seated at the right hand of God the Father almighty; from thence He shall come to judge the living and the dead. I believe in the Holy Spirit; the holy Catholic Church; the Communion of Saints; the forgiveness of sins; the resurrection of the body; and life everlasting. Amen.

Glory Be to the Father

Glory be to the Father, and to the Son, and to the Holy Spirit. As it was in the beginning, is now, and ever shall be, world without end. Amen.

Act of Faith

O my God, I believe that You are one God in three Divine Persons: Father, Son, and Holy Spirit. I believe that Your Divine Son became Man and died for our sins, and that He will come to judge the living and the dead. I believe these and all the truths that the Catholic Church teaches, because You have revealed them, who can neither deceive nor be deceived. Amen.

Act of Hope

O my God, relying on Your almighty power and infinite mercy and promises, I hope to obtain pardon of my sins, the help of Your grace, and life everlasting through the merits of Jesus Christ, my Lord and Redeemer. Amen.

Act of Love

O my God, I love You above all things with my whole heart and soul, because You are all good and worthy of all love. I love my neighbor as myself for the love of You. I forgive all who have injured me, and ask pardon of all whom I have injured. Amen.

Prayer to the Holy Spirit

Come, O Holy Spirit, fill the hearts of Your faithful and kindle in them the fire of Your love.

V. Send forth Your Spirit and they shall be created.

R. And You shall renew the face of the earth.

Let us pray: O God, who have taught the hearts of the faithful by the light of the Holy Spirit, grant that in the same Spirit, we may be always truly wise and ever rejoice in His consolation. Through Christ our Lord.

R. Amen.

Morning Prayer

Thank You, my loving Jesus, for bringing me to a new day. Give me strength to live this day totally for love of You, my Lord and my God.

As I begin this new day, I turn my thoughts to You in heaven, dear Jesus. I also think of You living in the tabernacle of my parish church. And finally, dear Jesus, I remember You are living by grace in my soul. How I love You, dear Jesus! I want to live and I want to die only for love of You!

Heavenly Mother Mary, watch over me this day. I am your child. I wear your scapular to show that you are my Mother.

Guardian angel of mine, guard and protect me today.

St._____, my patron saint, pray for me today.

My God — Father, Son, and Holy Spirit — I want to grow in grace today and serve Jesus in others.

Morning Offering

O Jesus, through the Immaculate Heart of Mary, I offer You my prayers, works, joys, and sufferings of this day in union with the holy Sacrifice of the Mass throughout the world. I offer them for all the intentions of Your Sacred Heart: the salvation of souls, reparation for sin, the reunion of all Christians. I offer them for the intentions of our bishops and of all members of the Apostleship of Prayer, and in particular for those recommended by our Holy Father this month.

Daily Offering

O my God, in union with the Immaculate Heart of Mary *(here kiss your Brown Scapular/Miraculous Medal),* I offer You the Precious Blood of Jesus from all the altars throughout the world, joining with it the offering of my every thought, word, and action of this day. O my Jesus, I desire today to gain every indulgence and merit I can, and I offer them, together with myself, to Mary Immaculate, that she may best apply them to the interests of Your most Sacred Heart.

Precious Blood of Jesus, save us!

Immaculate Heart of Mary, pray for us!
Sacred Heart of Jesus, have mercy on us!

Evening Prayer

O Blessed Trinity — Father, Son, and Holy Spirit — I come to the end of this day. I am one day closer to heaven. Thank You for all the joys and graces of this day. I beg pardon for my failures today. I now examine my conscience over this day.

(Recall any sins you may have committed today against God, and your failures to show love to others. How did you practice your Spiritual Program *today? See page 20.)*

(Recite the Act of Contrition.*)*

Be with me tonight, dear Lord. Watch over me while I sleep. Send Your holy angels, and especially my guardian angel, to protect me this night.

Bless my home, dear God above. I ask You to send Your special graces upon my parents and all the members of my family. *(Name them.)*

I ask my patron, St. _____, to continue prayers for my salvation, and that I may serve others for the love of God.

Heavenly Father, turn Your anger from people who are living in sin. Convert them to Your loving grace. Guard innocent souls. Help those tempted this night. Keep me from sin.

Comfort those in sorrow. Bless those who must die this night. Take them all to heaven. Give the souls in purgatory strength, and bring them to heaven soon.

Stay with me and my family, O Jesus, Good Shepherd, as we sleep this night. I want to renew my consecration to Your Sacred Heart, O Jesus, and to the Immaculate Heart of Mary, my spiritual Mother. Thank You for this day. Amen.

Prayer in the Evening
(By St. Augustine)

Watch, O Lord, with those who wake, or
    watch, or weep tonight, and give Your angels
    and saints charge over those who sleep.
Tend Your sick ones, O Lord Christ;
Rest Your weary ones;
Bless Your dying ones;
Soothe Your suffering ones;
Pity Your afflicted ones;
Shield Your joyous ones;
And all for Your love's sake. Amen.

PRAYERS DURING THE CHURCH YEAR

Advent

My God, I am waiting for the Christmas season. I want to celebrate the birthday of Jesus. I am thinking of those thousands of years when the world did not have Jesus, when the world was dark and in sin because it was without Jesus.

I thank You, God, for sending Abraham and Moses, Isaiah, and all the other prophets to get the world ready for Jesus. I thank You for sending John the Baptist. And most of all, dear God, I thank You for giving the world the Blessed Virgin Mary to prepare for Your coming.

I will pray extra hard during Advent, my God. I will get my soul ready for Jesus to come into it at Christmastime. Come, Lord Jesus, come. Amen.

Christmastime

Infant Jesus, I love You. You are now a babe. I believe You are the Son of God, born of the Virgin Mother, Mary. I believe, dear Jesus, that You came to this earth to teach us about God. I believe You came to place the Church upon earth to do Your work. And Jesus, I believe that You came to redeem us by dying on the Cross.

I see You in the crib, my Jesus. I think also of the Cross upon which You will die someday. Thank You, Jesus, for becoming a child like me in all things except sin. How much You loved us in heaven, that You have come down to our earth as a baby boy. Thank You, Jesus. Amen.

Lent

Lord God, this holy season of Lent is a time for me to do penance. My Jesus, You did penance for the whole world by Your death on the Cross. Men whipped Your sacred Body. They crowned You with big thorns, which were driven into Your sacred head. They made You carry the Cross up the hill of Calvary.

For three long hours You hung upon the Cross with spikes driven through Your feet and hands. You thirsted for souls. You shed Your precious Blood for the entire world and for me. During all Your sufferings, You saw my personal sins also. You suffered for me.

My Jesus, You said to each one of us, "Unless you take up your cross and follow Me, you cannot be My disciple." You also said, "Unless you do penance, you will all likewise perish." I cannot save my soul unless I do penance. Every Friday is a special day of penance, but now I want to do penance in union with You, Jesus, for the forty days of Lent.

My Jesus, I unite my special Lenten prayers and sacrifices to Your holy sufferings this Lent. Give me strength not to weaken or give up. I want to keep my will strong and do penance in Your love without fail. I shall keep carrying the cross and rise with You on Easter Sunday. Amen.

Easter Time

O risen Jesus, how happy I am and full of joy to be a Christian. You are risen. You are my Lord, God, and Savior. I know that my faith is true because You rose from the dead.

O Jesus, You rose again from the dead on the third day, just as You said You would. Because You have risen, I, too, will rise from the grave someday.

Thank You, dear Jesus, for dying on the Cross and rising from the dead to leave behind an empty tomb and linen cloths. My risen Jesus, I love You. I adore You. Amen.

The Ascension

After forty days on earth when You rose from the dead, dear Jesus, You ascended back into heaven. You let Yourself be seen by crowds of people, up to five hundred at a time. But then it was time for You to go back to heaven from which You came when You first descended into the sweet womb of Mary.

Before ascending into heaven, You told the Apostles to preach Your word and to baptize in the Name of the Father, and of the Son, and of the Holy Spirit. You promised that the Holy Spirit would come to the Apostles. I pray that the Holy Spirit will work in my soul, too. From Your throne in heaven, my Jesus, I ask of You, together with God the Father, to send the Holy Spirit into my soul and into the whole Church. Amen.

Pentecost

Dear Jesus, You kept Your promise. You and God the Father sent the Holy Spirit down upon the Church. God is love. The Spirit of Love came in the form of tongues of burning fire, and a mighty wind was heard. Christians must love, and they must speak of Your love to others. Send a tongue of Your fire, O Holy Spirit, into my soul. I want to love greatly. I want to speak of Your love, too.

Mary and the Apostles were filled with Your love, O Holy Spirit, on that first Pentecost. O Holy Spirit, You are the Spouse of Mary. Mary, you, too, can pray to have the Holy Spirit fill my soul with love. The Holy Spirit lives in the Church. I want the strength of the Holy Spirit to do the work of Jesus today. I want to be an apostle of Your word and Your love, O Jesus. Your Holy Spirit can give me that power. Amen.

Christ the King

Lord Jesus Christ, King of heaven and earth, I adore You profoundly. You are my King, the King of all people, of angels and saints. Lord of lords, and King of kings, I ask You to renew the whole world in Your love. The nations of the world have been torn apart by sin. I ask, O gentlest and most merciful King, that You bring all the families of nations under Your loving rule.

Jesus, You are King of all saints, in heaven, in purgatory, and on earth. You are presently in the Blessed Sacrament of our tabernacles, where you reign as a silent King. O heavenly King, You once laid down Your life for Your people. O King of love, I beg that I may enter Your heavenly kingdom one day to live with You forever and ever. Amen.

Friday

O Jesus, it was on a Friday that You shed Your precious Blood on the Cross and redeemed the world. You did penance for the entire world. Mother

Church asks that I set every Friday of the year aside as a special day of penance. This Friday I want to offer special prayers and sacrifices in reparation for my personal sins and those of the world.

O Jesus, there are so many things I can do in penance on Friday. I can give up things, like candy and pop; and the Church has asked that a first choice be to give up eating meat. I can visit the sick, the lonely; I can do special things to serve You in my neighbor. I want especially to remember that You are present in the Blessed Sacrament as a victim of love.

My Jesus, thank You for suffering so much for me on Good Friday. Accept this act of my love. Amen.

Saturday

Miraculous Queen of heaven, this is your special day of the week. Holy Mother the Church thinks of you, dear Mother of the Church, in a special way, each Saturday in preparation for the Lord's Day.

Today I desire to offer reparation to your Immaculate Heart and to bring comfort also to the Sacred Heart of your Son. For love of you, my Lady, for the conversion of sinners, I offer this entire day — all my thoughts, words, and actions. I shall try to pray my Rosary extra well, thinking on the mysteries.

Sweet heart of Mary, be my salvation as you lead me to your Son, Jesus Christ, who has redeemed the world. I wish to offer every day to your two hearts, but especially Saturday, which is for you, dear heavenly Mother.

Through your intercession, lead many souls from purgatory into heaven this day. Amen.

May

Queen of heaven, Queen of May, this is your special month. My Queen, my Mother, I love you so much. I am your child. I feel so full of life and happiness during this beautiful month of May.

It is spring. All nature is flowing with new life and beauty. The flowers are blooming. Mother Earth is taking on beautiful colors. The birds are happy. All God's creation is so beautiful. O Mother Mary, how beautiful you must be. You are more beautiful than all the beauty of the earth. You are more beautiful than all the angels and saints together. All the beauty of May speaks of you, Mary. Even the blue sky and white clouds remind me of your beautiful garments. The bright sun speaks of you, O Lady of light.

This May, O beautiful Lady of mine, I consecrate myself to you anew. Amen.

October

O Lady of the holy Rosary, this is your special month. It is October, and I am reminded how powerful the Rosary is. I love to pray the Rosary, for when I pray the Rosary, my Mother, I can lay so many roses at your feet. Each Hail Mary is another rose I give to you to present to Jesus, your Son and my Savior.

O my sweetest Mother Mary, I shall try to pray the Rosary well. I know you will help. By praying the

Rosary, I think of the important things in the life of Jesus. I praise the Blessed Trinity. I pray the Lord's Prayer. I even make a profession of Catholic faith as the Apostles did.

My Mother, I like to think of the Rosary, not only as roses I give to you, but also as a reminder of the truths of heaven. Through the Rosary, I shall pray that souls be saved.

This month of October, I come to you, O Queen of the Rosary, and ask for peace for the world. Through the Rosary I ask for all the things I need. Amen.

PRAYERS TO OUR LADY

Hail Mary

Hail Mary, full of grace, the Lord is with thee; blessed art thou among women, and blessed is the fruit of thy womb, Jesus.

Holy Mary, Mother of God, pray for us sinners, now and at the hour of our death. Amen.

Angelus

V. The angel of the Lord declared unto Mary.

R. And she conceived by the Holy Spirit. Hail Mary, etc.

V. Behold the handmaid of the Lord.

R. Be it done unto me according to your word. Hail Mary, etc.

V. And the Word was made flesh.
R. And dwelt among us. Hail Mary, etc.
V. Pray for us, O holy Mother of God.
R. That we may be made worthy of the promises of Christ.

Let us pray: Pour forth, we beseech You, O Lord, Your grace into our hearts, that we, to whom the Incarnation of Christ, Your Son, was made known by the message of an angel, may, by His Passion and Cross, be brought to the glory of His Resurrection. Through the same Christ our Lord.
R. Amen.

Regina Caeli

(During the Easter Season, the Regina Caeli *replaces the* Angelus.*)*

V. Queen of heaven, rejoice, alleluia.
R. For He whom you did merit to bear, alleluia.
V. Has risen as He said, alleluia.
R. Pray for us to God, alleluia.
V. Rejoice and be glad, O Virgin Mary, alleluia.
R. For the Lord is truly risen, alleluia.

Let us pray: O God, who gave joy to the world through the Resurrection of Your Son, our Lord Jesus Christ, grant, we beseech You, that through the intercession of the Virgin Mary, His Mother, we may obtain the joys of everlasting life. Through the same Christ our Lord.

R. Amen.

Prayer to Our Mother of Grace

O Immaculate Mother of grace, God wills to give grace through you. Jesus is the Savior. Jesus earned all grace for us by His life, death, and Resurrection. And yet, Immaculate Mary, God the Father has willed for you to lead us to Jesus, to the throne of grace.

O Immaculate Heart of Mary, ask Jesus to give my soul many graces. Also, sweet heart of Mary, I ask you to grant graces for the conversion of sinners. Keep me always in the grace of your Son, Jesus Christ. Jesus, Mary, I love you. Save souls. Amen.

Prayer to Mary as Mother

Mary, never to an angel have you said, "You are my child!" Yet, because you are the Mother of the Church and I am a member of the Mystical Body of Jesus, you are my Mother and I am your child.

Mary, my Mother, I am your little child. I know I am not much, but your love makes me know how important you consider my soul and the soul of everyone. I am weak. I need the support of your arms, and I need to have you keep me in your Immaculate Heart. Keep me from the evil of Satan.

Guide me and protect me. Amen.

Prayer to the Mother of the Church

How wonderful it is to live in the house of the Lord all the days of my life. Mary, you are the Mother of the Church. When Jesus was dying on the Cross, He looked down at you and at John the Apostle. Your Son, Jesus, said to you, "Behold your son." How happy I am that St. John took the place of everyone in the Church when Jesus said to him, "Behold your Mother."

O Mary, you are the Mother of Jesus and all the members of His Church. Jesus has earned all grace, and through you He gives His divine life to our souls.

MOTHER OF THE WORD,
by Mark Sanislo (Fiat Studios, Coon
Rapids, Minnesota)

How happy I am to be a member of the Church and have you for my Mother. I love you. Amen.

Prayer to Mary, Mother of Grace
(From the Roman Ritual)

Mary, Mother of grace,
Mother of mercy,
Shield me from the enemy
And receive me at the hour of my death.

Prayer to Mary to Help the Helpless
(From the Roman Breviary)

Holy Mary, help the helpless, strengthen the fearful, comfort the sorrowful, pray for the people, plead for the clergy, intercede for all women consecrated to God; may all who keep your sacred commemoration experience the might of your assistance.

Prayer to Mary, Queen of Angels

O Mary, heavenly Queen of all the angels, I give to you my love. My Queen, my Mother, send the angels of heaven to watch over the Church. Send the nine choirs of heavenly angels to lead the world to peace. O Queen of angels, extend your love in a special way to my guardian angel, and ask him to watch over and protect me so that I may always live in grace. I ask you, O heavenly Queen, to accept from my guardian angel, from St. Gabriel, St. Michael, St. Raphael, and all the other angels, my profoundest expression of love for you and your Son, Jesus Christ. Amen.

Prayer to Mary, Mother of Mercy

Mary, Mother of mercy, I give you my heart and my soul. I ask that you give to me the kindest expression of your mercy.

My Mother, my mercy, I have offended your Son, Jesus Christ, many times by my sins. In offending the Sacred Heart of your Son, I have sinned against your Immaculate Heart as well. I have caused you sorrow when I have wounded the heart of your Son. But you are a mother of compassion and of love. Through your prayers, O gentle Mother of mercy, I implore the forgiveness and mercy of your Son, Jesus Christ.

Mother of mercy, obtain forgiveness and peace for the whole world. Amen.

Prayer to Our Lady of Atonement

Blessed Lady of heaven, together with your Son, Jesus Christ, you will that all Christians may be one, just as your Son is one with God the Father. I wish to offer to God the Father, in the unity of the Holy Spirit, the offering you made of your Son's suffering and death on the Cross. I wish to offer your own faith and love and sorrow, which you showed as you stood beneath the Cross on Calvary.

O Lady of atonement, I wish to join my own poor prayers and sacrifices to those you knew so well on earth. For this and in this way, I ask your prayers again that all Christians may be one in faith. May all be of one fold and one Shepherd. Amen.

Prayer to Our Lady of the Rosary

Mary, Our Lady of the Rosary, I want to love your Immaculate Heart and think on the things of your Son, Jesus Christ, while praying the most holy Rosary. When I pray the Rosary, I will think of the mysteries of the life of Jesus. Thank you, O Mary, for giving us the Rosary, by which I can give spiritual roses to your Immaculate Heart. Then, too, by the Rosary, I can remove thorns from the Heart of your Son.

O Queen of the holy Rosary, you have promised that you will give us everything we ask for from your Son when we ask through the praying of your Rosary. By the Rosary, I ask for peace for the world, for all souls to go to heaven. I ask, too, that God be known and loved everywhere. Amen.

Prayer to Our Lady of Guadalupe

O Lady of Guadalupe, who appeared to St. Juan Diego near Mexico City in 1531 and left the most beautiful picture of yourself on his clothing, I come before you as your little child. I ask you to show me and every person all of your love, your compassion, your help. Show your protection to all persons.

O Lady of Guadalupe, great lover of all peoples, you who have shown your special love for the Americas, I ask you to hear our weeping. Bring comfort to our sorrows, our needs, our miseries.

I am just a little child, but I ask you, O merciful Mother, to give me a big heart with which to love you, to love your Son, Jesus, and to love everyone. Thank you. Amen.

Prayer to Our Lady of Lourdes

O Lady of Lourdes, you who appeared in 1858 to a fourteen-year-old girl, St. Bernadette, I come to honor you and your Immaculate Conception. O Mary, God created you without original sin. You never committed the slightest sin in your whole life. O how good, pure, and holy you are. At Lourdes you said: "I am the Immaculate Conception."

Sweet Lady of Lourdes, I shall try to do what you told St. Bernadette: "Pray and do penance for the conversion of the world." Thank you for giving the world the special waters at Lourdes. May those waters remind us of our baptism as children of God.

O Immaculate Conception, you smiled often at Lourdes. Smile now upon the Church. Give peace to souls and to the whole world. Amen.

Prayer to Mary, Mediatrix of All Graces

O Blessed Virgin Mary, through the power of the Holy Spirit, give the graces of your Son, Jesus Christ, to my soul and all souls. God became Man in Jesus Christ, O Mary, through the action of your holy will and body. Our Lord Jesus Christ was first known and loved in your Immaculate Heart, and then He became the sweet fruit of your womb.

By the Redemption of Jesus Christ, by the shedding of His most precious Blood to save souls, and by your own sorrows and sufferings, O Mary, I come to the heavenly throne of God. I am God's child and yours, O Mary. Fill my soul with heavenly grace. Amen.

Prayer to Our Lady of the Miraculous Medal

"O Mary, conceived without sin, pray for us who have recourse to you." Thank you, Mary, for giving St. Catherine Labouré the Miraculous Medal in 1830.

O Lady of the Miraculous Medal, you have reminded us by your crowning with twelve stars that you are the Queen of the Apostles. By the Cross, you have reminded us that your Son, Jesus Christ, saved the world by shedding His precious Blood.

By the Sacred Heart of your Son, and by your Immaculate Heart, dear Mother, I ask always for the protection of heaven. Amen.

Prayer to Our Lady of the Most Blessed Sacrament

Mother of Jesus, you are our perfect model of one who adored Jesus in the Most Blessed Sacrament. The same Jesus Christ, true God and true Man, whom you brought into the world, lives in the Most Blessed Sacrament. Mary, Jesus gave you to the care of St. John the Apostle. From the time of the death of Jesus on the Cross, you went to live with the priest

John. Oh, with what reverence St. John offered the holy Sacrifice of the Mass, and you, Our Lady, joined in adoring your Son as He became present in the Most Blessed Sacrament.

Inspire me, my Lady, to adore your Son, Jesus, in the Most Blessed Sacrament as you did. You carried the Lord Jesus in your holy womb. You were the first tabernacle to hold Jesus. With your words, "Be it done to me," you brought Jesus to earth for the first time when the angel Gabriel appeared to you. Today the Catholic priest says, "This is My Body. . . . This is My Blood." The priest, like you, brings Jesus to earth again in the Most Blessed Sacrament. And you, my Mother Mary, are still the Mother of Jesus in the Sacrament of the Altar. I offer Jesus the most pure and perfect love that you showed Him when you adored Him in this Sacrament of Love. O Lady of the Most Blessed Sacrament, pray for me now and at the hour of my death. Amen.

Prayer to the Queen of the Risen Jesus

How happy you were that first Easter Sunday, O Queen of heaven, when Jesus appeared to you. Jesus rose from the dead as He said He would. Just as Jesus thought last of you as He hung dying on the Cross, so Jesus thought first of you when He rose from the grave. O Mary, I join in your joy of the risen Jesus. Alleluia.

Your body is in heaven now, O Mary, together with your soul. God took you into heaven, in both body and soul. Jesus rose from the dead and ascended into heaven. Now Jesus lives in heaven, seated next to His heavenly Father in the unity of the Holy Spirit. There you are, too, O Mary, Mother of the risen Jesus.

Just as Jesus lives now to pray for us, so you, too, Mary, live now in heaven. Together with the risen Jesus, pray for us who are the children of God, the brothers and sisters of Jesus, and your children still upon earth. Amen.

Prayer to Our Lady, Help of Christians

O heavenly Lady, help of Christians, I come to you, for you never refuse help to anyone. Mary, help of Christians, you have often answered the prayers of nations. You have helped the Pope, bishops, priests, religious, and all Christians. Whenever those who love you put their hope in you, you hurry to them with a mother's love. Your greatest wish is to help the holy Church of your Son still here on earth.

My Mother, my hope, O Lady, help of Christians, make me live in the love of your holy Son, Jesus Christ. Help me in my every need. Amen.

Hail, Holy Queen

Hail, holy Queen, Mother of mercy! Hail, our life, our sweetness, and our hope! To you do we cry, poor banished children of Eve; to you do we send up our sighs, mourning, and weeping in this valley of tears!

Turn then, most gracious advocate, your eyes of mercy toward us; and after this, our exile, show unto us the blessed fruit of your womb, Jesus. O clement, O loving, O sweet Virgin Mary.

The Memorare

Remember, O most gracious Virgin Mary, that never was it known that anyone who fled to your protection, implored your help, or sought your intercession was left unaided. Inspired by this confidence, I fly unto you, O Virgin of virgins, my Mother. To you I come, before you I stand, sinful and sorrowful. O Mother of the Word Incarnate, despise not my petitions, but in your mercy hear and answer me. Amen.

The Magnificat

(Mary herself prayed this prayer. It is found in Luke 1:46-55.)

My soul proclaims the greatness of the Lord and my spirit exults in God my Savior; because He has looked upon His lowly handmaid.

Yes, from this day forward all generations will call me blessed, for the Almighty has done great things for me. Holy is His Name, and His mercy reaches from age to age for those who fear Him.

He has shown the power of His arm, He has routed the proud of heart. He has pulled down princes from their thrones and exalted the lowly. The hungry He has filled with good things, the rich sent empty away.

He has come to the help of Israel His servant, mindful of His mercy — according to the promise He made to our ancestors — of His mercy to Abraham and to his descendants forever.

Seven Hail Marys in Honor of the Seven Sorrows of Mary

Mary has promised very special graces to those who do this on a daily basis. Included in the promises of Our Lady for those who practice this devotion is her pledge to give special assistance at the hour of death, including the sight of her face. These are the seven sorrows:

- **The First Sorrow:** The Prophecy of Simeon (Hail Mary).
- **The Second Sorrow:** The Flight Into Egypt (Hail Mary).
- **The Third Sorrow:** The Loss of the Child Jesus in the Temple (Hail Mary).
- **The Fourth Sorrow:** Jesus and Mary Meet on the Way to the Cross (Hail Mary).
- **The Fifth Sorrow:** Jesus Dies on the Cross (Hail Mary).
- **The Sixth Sorrow:** Jesus Is Taken Down From the Cross and Laid in the Arms of Mary (Hail Mary).
- **The Seventh Sorrow:** The Burial of Jesus (Hail Mary).

Prayers to the Sacred Heart and Immaculate Heart

To Jesus' Heart All Burning

How I love You, Jesus. Your Sacred Heart is burning with love for me. I know that You love me and all persons so much. Too often we hurt You with our sins. Too often have I put thorns into Your holy heart by sin. I am sorry, O Sacred Heart of Jesus.

Jesus, You love me and all people. You ask us to love You as You love us. I know I could never love You that much, Jesus. I will try. I ask You to give me Your heart and soul to love the way You love.

Dear Jesus, I ask pardon for all the sins committed against You. I promise to work hard to love You and to get others to love You. Amen.

To Jesus' Heart Wounded

Jesus, I see You saddened at the sins of people. My sins have wounded You, too. When You hung dying on the Cross, Your Sacred Heart felt more hurt by the sins of people than by the nails and whips and thorns.

The Sacred Heart

O Sacred Heart of Jesus, what can I do to make up for being so cold and not thanking You enough for loving me and everyone so much? From now on I'll try harder not to wound Your heart with sin. I'll try to keep others from putting thorns into Your heart and soul. I'll work so that others will know You and see how much You love them. Amen.

To the Heart of Mary Burning With Love

O Mary, I see that your Immaculate Heart burns with love like that of Jesus. It is Jesus who is the Savior of the world. You, Mary, are the Mother of the world's Savior. Thank you, Mary, for giving us Jesus. Thank you for saying "yes" when God asked you to be His Mother and our Mother.

Your heart, O Immaculate Mother, is aflame with love set ablaze by the love of Jesus. You, Mary, love each one of us as a child. I know that you also want me to love Jesus with all my heart and soul. Mary, teach me to love Jesus with the kind of love with which your Immaculate Heart burned for love of your Son. Amen.

To the Immaculate Heart of Mary Wounded by Sin

O sorrowful and Immaculate Heart of Mary, your heart, too, is wounded by the sins of people. What people do by sin to the heart of Jesus they do to you, too. Your heart is so sad because people are turning away from Jesus and not loving Him. At least, Mary, I will try to love as I should. I will try to get others to love you and Jesus.

O Immaculate Heart of Mary, I offer this prayer and my daily work and cares to you in reparation for the sins committed against your Son. Take this offering of my love. Give it to Jesus with your own pure heart. Amen.

To the Sorrowful and Immaculate Heart of Mary

O Mary, just as the prophet Simeon had foretold, a sword of sorrow pierced your soul. You are a kind and tender mother. What hurts your Son, hurts your Immaculate Heart, too.

O Mother, my dearest Mother, I wish to console you for the sins of the world. I am sorry, too, for the sins I have committed. I wish to make reparation so as to satisfy for sin, which wounds your sorrowful and Immaculate Heart. Sweet heart of Mary, be my salvation. Amen.

To the Two Hearts

O Sacred Heart of Jesus and Immaculate Heart of Mary, to your two hearts do I come to beg for the infinite merits and graces that only God can give. It was the love of Your Sacred Heart, O Jesus, that gave us Yourself in Holy Communion. It was Your love that caused You to die on the Cross and redeem the world.

Mary, you joined the love of your Immaculate Heart to every thought, word, and deed of Jesus.

Your heart always beat as one with the heart of Jesus. Even now, your heart is tenderly joined in heaven to the love of Jesus so as to save the world.

O Mary, teach me to love Jesus as you do. With your Immaculate Heart, O Mary, and with Your Sacred Heart, Lord Jesus, I present your combined love — and the precious Blood You shed, Jesus — to the heavenly Father in reparation for my sins and the sins of the whole world. Amen.

PRAYERS FOR THE SACRIFICE OF THE MASS

Offering of the Body and Blood of Jesus to God

O Body and Blood of Jesus Christ, horribly insulted by ungrateful men, I wish to make reparation for their crimes and to console my God. I give You my heart and my soul. I offer all that I am, and I join myself to Jesus. I offer to You my work, my study, my play, my prayers. Above all, I offer to God my Father the precious Body and Blood of Jesus, which He once offered on the Cross. Amen.

Prayer to Jesus the Priest
(Before Mass)

O Jesus, I have come to holy Mass. You are our High Priest. You will offer the Sacrifice of the Mass. On Good Friday You died on the Cross. You died for the sins of the whole world. By the sacrifice of Your death, You opened the gates of heaven for us. What

You did on the Cross, my loving Jesus, You will make present here again on this altar. It is just as if I were present at the altar of the Cross that first Good Friday. Now You will not feel the pain. But Jesus, at this holy Mass You shall offer the same sacrifice. You will again be the Priest at this Mass. The love You gave God the Father and the whole world You will give at this Mass. Thank You, Jesus, for bringing me here to have a part. Thank You for being the Priest of this Mass. Amen.

Prayer to Jesus as Victim
(Before Mass)

Jesus, I believe that the holy Mass is a sacrifice. A victim is needed, to be offered as a gift to God. Long ago people offered animals, grain, oil, and such things to You as sacrifice. God, our heavenly Father, wanted a perfect sacrifice. So, instead of the things of this earth, our Father sent You, Jesus, from heaven to earth. From Mary, through the power of the Holy Spirit, You took a body like mine. But still, Jesus, You were God. With Your Body You carried the heavy Cross up the hill of Calvary. There You let men nail You to the Cross. It was the sins of the world that nailed You to the Cross. My sins did that, too. Nailed to the Cross, You became a victim of sacrifice.

Jesus, just as You shed Your precious Blood on the Cross to save the world, now in this Mass You will offer Your Blood. At this Mass I, too, shall offer our heavenly Father Your precious Body and Blood. Thank You, Jesus, for being the perfect Gift and Victim we can offer for our sins and those of the whole world. Amen.

Prayer to Jesus Whom I Will Receive in Holy Communion

Jesus, I believe that I will receive You in Holy Communion. It is really You who will come into my heart and soul. I must get ready now. I must have a clean heart and a pure soul. Forgive me for whatever sins I have committed against You. I am sorry. I want to be joined to You always, my Jesus.

I want to open my heart and soul wide to receive You. I love You. I want You to fill my soul with Your grace. I want Your life to come into my soul. I want to live with You forever in heaven. I am not worthy to receive You. You can make me worthy. I love You with all my heart and soul. Come to me, O Jesus, as I come to You. Amen.

Prayer to Jesus in the Blessed Sacrament

Jesus, I've come to holy Mass. I want to receive You in Holy Communion at this Mass. I believe that Your priest shall change the bread and wine into Your sacred Body and Blood. I believe that You, Jesus, are really present in the host and in the chalice the priest lifts up at Mass. I shall look up at the sacred host and the chalice and whisper, "My Lord and my God."

I want my soul to be as clean as possible to receive You at this Mass. I am sorry for whatever sins I have committed to hurt Your Sacred Heart, O Jesus. I am sorry I didn't stop to think how wrong I was acting at the times I sinned; but now I come to You in faith and in love. I want You, Jesus, to come to me. I want You to come into my soul. I want You to fill my heart with Your love and Your grace. I want to adore You forever in heaven. Amen.

PRAYERS FOLLOWING MASS AND HOLY COMMUNION

Say one or more of these prayers before leaving church. It is good, if possible, to remain in church for a while after Mass.

To Live With Jesus in Heaven

My Jesus, I love You. I adore You. You have come to me. I am one with You. You are now in my soul. How can I ever leave You again? I want You to stay with me, and in me, forever. I am so anxious to live with You forever in heaven. My Jesus, thank You. Thank You for coming into my soul to give me Your divine life. I want always to receive You. Amen.

To Offer Communion in Reparation

My Jesus, You are so good to me. I love You. Keep me; guard me as Your property and possession.

Fill me with Your grace. Never let me fall into sin again. I want to offer this Holy Communion in reparation for all the sins committed against Your Sacred Heart and the Immaculate Heart of Your holy Mother. Jesus, I want to be holy and pure like Your Mother. Amen.

To Convert Poor Sinners

Jesus, You are with me. You are in me. My soul is now Your home. How can I ever love You enough for coming to me like this? I want to love You and everyone. I want always to be holy like You. I want to ask the Immaculate Heart of Your Mother, Mary, and my spiritual Mother, to pray for poor sinners. Convert them and save them from hell. Amen.

To Bless and Help Others

O Jesus, bless my parents and everyone. Bless my brothers and sisters, my friends, my teachers, our priests, bishops, the Pope, and all religious. Help all the children of the world to know and love You better. I want children of the world who do not know You to come to Your love. I want them to have the knowledge of Your holy Name. O my Jesus, I am not worthy that You should come to me; say only the word and my soul shall be healed. Amen.

To Renew Consecration

Now that You are in my heart, dear Jesus, I want to renew my consecration to Your Sacred Heart and to the Immaculate Heart of Your Mother, Mary. I am Yours, and Yours I want to be. Everything I am and have I give to You, my Jesus, and to my Mother, Mary. Take my prayers, good works, joys, everything. I give my life to You. Amen.

To Raise Up Our Bodies

Jesus, You have said, "He who eats My Body and drinks My Blood, I will raise him up on the last day." I believe that You shall raise my body up gloriously at the end of the world because I receive You in love in Holy Communion. Amen.

For the Poor Souls

Jesus, You are in my soul at this very moment. Your Body, Blood, Soul, and Divinity live within me. I offer this Holy Communion for the suffering souls in purgatory. Take them to heaven soon. Since they cannot receive You in Holy Communion anymore, I offer this Holy Communion for them and especially for _____. Amen.

To Show Love for Jesus

Jesus, You have come to my soul with all Your love. I want to give back to You the love that You have for me. I know that I can never do it well enough. I offer to You, then, the love with which Mary loved You upon earth and loves You even now in heaven.

I love You above all things, my Jesus. I am all Yours, and all I have is Yours, O loving Jesus, through Mary, Your Immaculate Mother. Amen.

Before a Crucifix

Look down upon me, good and gentle Jesus, while before Your face I humbly kneel and with burning soul pray and beseech You to fix deep in my heart lively sentiments of faith, hope, and charity, true contrition for my sins, and a firm purpose of amendment.

While I contemplate, with great love and tender pity, Your five most precious wounds, pondering over them within me and calling to mind the words that David, Your prophet, said of You, my Jesus:

"They have pierced My hands and My feet, they have numbered all My bones." Amen.

Soul of Christ (*Anima Christi*)

Soul of Christ, sanctify me.
Body of Christ, save me.
Blood of Christ, inebriate me.
Water from the side of Christ, wash me.
Passion of Christ, strengthen me.
O good Jesus, hear me.
Within Your wounds, hide me.
Separated from You, let me never be.
From the malignant enemy, defend me.
At the hour of death, call me.
To come to You, bid me,

That I may praise You in the company
Of Your saints, for all eternity. Amen.

To the Hidden Jesus

O Jesus, You who hide Yourself under the forms
of bread and wine, I adore You. You are now truly in
my heart under the veil of the Holy Eucharist. Sight,
taste, touch cannot tell what I have received. But I
trust my ears, dear Jesus. By faith I know that I have
You, my hidden God, within me. You have said it,
Jesus, and You are God the Son. I believe and I adore.
Amen.

Prayers for Benediction

Down in Adoration Falling

Down in adoration falling,
Lo! the sacred host we hail;
Lo! o'er ancient forms departing,
Newer rites of grace prevail;
Faith for all defects supplying,
Where the feeble senses fail.

To the everlasting Father,
And the Son who reigns on high,
With the Holy Spirit proceeding
Forth from each eternally,
Be salvation, honor, blessing,
Might, and endless majesty. Amen.

V. You have given them bread from heaven.

R. Having all sweetness within it.

Let us pray: O God, who in this wonderful Sacrament left us a memorial of Your Passion, grant, we implore You, that we may so venerate the sacred mysteries of Your Body and Blood as always to be conscious of the fruit of Your Redemption. You who live and reign forever and ever.

R. Amen.

The Divine Praises

Blessed be God.

Blessed be His holy Name.

Blessed be Jesus Christ, true God and true Man.

Blessed be the Name of Jesus.

Blessed be His most Sacred Heart.

Blessed be His most precious Blood.

Blessed be Jesus in the most holy Sacrament of the Altar.

Blessed be the Holy Spirit, the Paraclete.

Blessed be the great Mother of God, Mary most holy.

Blessed be her holy and Immaculate Conception.

Blessed be her glorious Assumption.

Blessed be the name of Mary, Virgin and Mother.

Blessed be St. Joseph, her most chaste spouse.

Blessed be God in His angels and in His saints.

May the heart of Jesus, in the Most Blessed Sacrament, be praised, adored, and loved with grateful affection, at every moment, in all the tabernacles of the world, even to the end of time. Amen.

Prayers for Spiritual Communion

An Act of Spiritual Communion
(From the Enchiridion)

My Jesus, I believe that You are in the Blessed Sacrament. I love You above all things, and I long for You in my soul. Since I cannot now receive You sacramentally, come at least spiritually into my heart. As though You have already come, I embrace You and unite myself entirely to You; never permit me to be separated from You. Amen.

A Spiritual Communion

My Jesus, I cannot now receive You in Holy Communion. I would like to have You come into my heart and soul in the Sacrament of the Holy Eucharist. But that is not possible now, dear Jesus. And so, I come to You, dear Jesus, to ask You to come to me spiritually.

Come to me, O Jesus, as I come to You. Fill my heart and my soul with Your love. Put Your holy grace into my soul. Make me know that You are present and that You forgive whatever sins I have committed.

I love You, dear Jesus. I want always to be with You and in You, and for You to be in me. Come, Lord Jesus, come to me. Amen.

CONFESSION

Prayer Before Confession

Holy Spirit, help me to remember my sins and to be sorry for them. I am sorry for my sins because they have offended You, my God. Jesus, I see You being scourged at the pillar. Men pound a crown of thorns into Your sacred head. They nail You to the Cross. You hang there suffering for three long hours before You die. My sins did these things to You, too.

I will try hard to make a good confession in reparation for my sins and those of the world.

I love You, O Sacred Heart of Jesus. I never want to offend You again. But I am so weak, O Lord. You must help me. I cannot stay out of sin without Your help. I will try hard. I will pray to You when I am tempted.

Now I will examine my conscience. *(See* Examination of Conscience, *page 64.)*

Prayer After Confession

O Jesus, thank You for forgiving my sins. How happy I am to be in Your grace. Now I have Your divine life in my soul more fully. You have forgiven my sins. I thank You for being so full of mercy for me, a sinner. I love You now, more than ever before. I want to stay clean in soul.

My Jesus, I think of You present in the Most Blessed Sacrament of the tabernacle. I adore You. I believe in You. I hope in You. I beg pardon for those who do not believe in You, do not adore You, do not hope in You, and do not love You.

Now I will say my penance to help take away the temporal punishment due to the sins You have forgiven.

Manner of Going to Confession

Before Confession

How to prepare for confession:

- Pray to the Holy Spirit — to know my sins and to be sorry for them. *(See* Prayer to the Holy Spirit, *page 25.)*
- Think of my sins — and how often I did them. *(See* Examination of Conscience, *page 64.)*
- Be sorry for my sins — think of how Jesus suffered on the Cross because of them. *(Then say the* Act of Contrition, *page 67.)*
- Promise to try not to sin again — because I love Jesus so much and fear punishment if I do not have my sins forgiven.
- Think — I will listen carefully to what Father tells me in the confessional and will remember to do the penance he gives me.

During Confession

How to go to confession:

- When the priest opens the slide to the confessional small door — or when I sit down, going face-to-face — I will begin by making the Sign of the Cross, saying: "Bless me, Father. My last confession was _____ ago. I am a/an _____-grade boy/girl."
- "These are my sins. . . ." I will be sure to state as best I can what I did and how many times I committed each. If I cannot remember just how many times, I will say, "About _____ times."
- Then I will say, "I am sorry for these and all the sins of my past life that I may have forgotten."
- Then I must listen to what Father says and listen extra hard to hear the penance he gives me.
- When Father is through and I am ready to leave, I will say, "Thank you, Father." Then I will go into the church and do my penance.

After Confession

I now must very carefully do the penance the priest has given me. I also may spend some time talking to Jesus in the Most Blessed Sacrament, telling Him that I love Him and want to keep good and close to Him and to His Mother, Mary.

Examination of Conscience

- **First Commandment:** *I am the Lord your God. You shall not have strange gods before Me.* Did I remember to love and adore God each day? Did I study my religion homework, pay attention in catechism class, and try my best to listen to Father at Mass? Did I remember to say my daily prayers? Did I show special respect for priests, religious, and teachers? Did I observe Friday as a special day of penance? Was I late for Mass on Sundays through my own fault, or deliberately leave early? Do I pray for the souls in purgatory? Do I show honor to the Blessed Virgin Mary, angels, and saints?

- **Second Commandment:** *You shall not take the Name of the Lord your God in vain.* Did I use the Name of God, the name of His Holy Mother, or the names of saints in the wrong way? Did I curse and call others bad names?

- **Third Commandment:** *Remember to keep holy the Lord's Day.* Did I miss holy Mass on Sunday or on a holy day of obligation through my own fault? (Saturday night Mass is considered part of the Lord's Day, if one wishes to go to Mass then instead of Sunday.) Did I pray the best I could at Mass? Did I worship in wrong — non-Catholic — churches? Did I do unnecessary physical work on Sunday that I should have done another day? Did I try to make all of Sunday a special day for

God? Did I fast one hour before Communion time? Did I make a good thanksgiving after Holy Communion? Did I distract others at Mass?

- **Fourth Commandment:** *Honor your father and your mother.* Did I obey and honor my parents, teachers, and priest? Did I sass older people who have authority over me? Did I show disrespect to older people in any way? Did I talk kindly to my parents, sometimes telling them about my day? Do I ever offer to help around the house, yard, farm, or with special church activities? Am I cheerful at school, home, and neighborhood? Do I ever show others, especially my parents, that I love them? Was I grumpy and not enjoying the things the family usually does together? Did I join in family prayers? Did I remind the members of my family to pray if they forgot? Did I pay attention to my teacher in school?

- **Fifth Commandment:** *You shall not kill.* Did I wish evil on someone? Did I fight with anyone? Did I become angry and lose my temper? Did I try to get even with someone? Do I help my schoolmates in an honest way? Do I dislike those who get better grades than I do? Do I look down on those who don't do as well as I do? Do I try to show special kindness to boys and girls who are lonely and poor, who find things hard? Do I make fun of others' mistakes? Do I get jealous of others who receive praise, clothes, or other things? Am I polite to everyone? Do I respect others' feelings? Do I share my toys with other boys and girls? Am I a bully?

- **Sixth Commandment:** *You shall not commit adultery.* Did I say bad or dirty words? Did I think dirty, unclean thoughts? Did I go to bad movies or watch bad television shows? Did I do an impure act alone, or with another? Did I dress in an immodest way? Did I tell dirty stories or jokes? Did I read bad things or look at dirty pictures?

- **Seventh Commandment:** *You shall not steal.* Did I steal anything? What did I steal? If I stole, did I give back what I stole, or do I intend to return it soon? Did I harm or destroy the property of others? Did I borrow something and not give it back? If I have a job for which I am paid, do I perform my work as I should?

- **Eighth Commandment:** *You shall not bear false witness against your neighbor.* Did I tell a lie to anyone? Did I say bad or uncharitable things about someone, even if I thought they were true things? Did I harm the good name or reputation of another by bad or uncharitable talk?

- **Ninth Commandment:** *You shall not covet your neighbor's wife.* Did I look at another in an unclean or covetous way? Do I appreciate the holiness of marriage of my parents and other husbands and wives? Do I pray for my parents to be always a good mother and father? Am I proud of my parents and thankful to God that I have them?

- **Tenth Commandment:** *You shall not covet your neighbor's goods.* Was I greedy and selfish and wanting what others had? Did I refuse to share? Was I kind and willing to play with another child who wanted to play with me? Did I dominate others while at play, in school, or at home?

Act of Contrition

O my God, I am heartily sorry for having offended You, and I detest all my sins, because of Your just punishments, but most of all because they offend You, my God, who are all good and deserving of all my love. I firmly resolve, with the help of Your grace, to sin no more and to avoid the near occasions of sin. Amen.

PRAYERS OF PETITION

For the Pope

Jesus, You made St. Peter the first Pope when You were still on earth. I believe that the Pope is the Holy Father for the whole world. The Pope is the Rock upon which You built Your holy Church, and You promised that it would last until the end of the world. Give our Pope the strength he needs to teach us rightly.

Jesus, the Pope must suffer much when people disobey Your teachings. You gave us the Pope to speak in Your Name. The Pope is the visible head of the

Church on earth, as You, Jesus, are the invisible Head in heaven. Give the Pope strength of health and wisdom of soul, to guide us always with the help of the Holy Spirit. Amen.

For Bishops

Jesus, You ordained the Apostles the first bishops and priests of the Church. Bishops have the *fullness* of Your holy priesthood and can ordain other priests. Together with and under the Pope, as successors of the Apostles, they teach, sanctify, and govern the Church.

Give all bishops the grace to be true apostles of Jesus Christ. While they must be administrators, at the same time keep them focused on Jesus Christ and His Gospel. Give them the courage to correct every abuse against faith and morals.

Their work and duties are great and difficult, but You, dear Jesus, have conquered the world. Give all bishops, and my (arch)bishop, the strength and perseverance that are needed. Amen.

For Christian Unity

My Jesus, at the Last Supper, You prayed that all Your followers would always be one. The night before You died on the Cross You prayed to God the Father that all members of the Church would be one, just as You and God the Father are one.

Today, dear Jesus, the members of Your Church are divided into hundreds of different groups. That is not Your will. You want us all to be one. We are to be one in faith, one in baptism, just as You are one Lord.

Dear Jesus, I shall do all I can so that all Christians will love one another. I will work and pray that Your will be done. You want one fold and one Shepherd. Bring all Christians together, dear Lord, into the unity of Your Church. Amen.

For the Church

Jesus, Lord, God and Savior, keep Your Church always in truth. Protect it and make it grow every day in new members so that all may come to save their souls.

Dear Jesus, You are the invisible Head of the Church. You are so close to the Church that the Bible calls the Church Your Body. You are the Vine, and we are the branches. You have said that no one can come to God the Father except through You. And dear Jesus, Your Church on earth is Your Body and the way You live in the world today. You love the Church. Keep all members of the Church in Your love. Make our faith and hope stronger.

Dear Jesus, just as some hated You in Your physical Body when You were on earth, so now, some hate You in Your Church, Your Mystical Body. I ask our heavenly Father, in Your Name, Jesus, and in the unity of the Holy Spirit, to protect holy Mother Church for the glory of God and the salvation of souls. Amen.

For Our Country

Dear God, bless our country, the United States of America. Keep our country in the Christian faith. Keep our country and all its peoples living in justice. Keep the young people of this great land noble, brave, loyal, and true.

Immaculate Heart of Mary, Mother of God, under your very special title of the Immaculate Conception, you are the patroness of the United States of America. Pray to your Divine Son, Jesus Christ, and with that special power you have, O Mary, by being always perfectly sinless, bring everyone in our country to Jesus Christ. Amen.

For Parents

Thank You, dear God, for giving me the very best parents. They are the best for me. Help me to love and obey my parents as I should. Give my parents a long life upon this earth. Lead them to heaven. Help my parents in all they need to provide a good home. May I never hurt You, dear God, or my parents, by becoming careless in my holy faith. Amen.

For Grandparents

Almighty God, Creator of heaven and earth and all people, thank You for the grandparents You have given me. Thank You for giving good parents to my mother and father.

I want You to bless my grandparents, dear God. I want them to live to a happy old age and then spend eternity with You in heaven. Good St. Anne, mother of the Blessed Virgin Mary, and St. Joachim, father of Mary, you were the grandparents of Jesus. Pray for my grandparents. Amen.

For One's Religion Teacher

Dear Jesus, You were the perfect Teacher. Your holy Mother, Mary, was a catechist, too. I want You, Jesus, and you, my Mother, Mary, to guide my teacher of religion as he (she) leads me in the way that leads to God.

Thank You, God, for giving my teacher a spirit of faith and love so as to help me. Send down Your special blessings upon my teacher of religion. Help me to respond so that I may grow more and more in faith, hope, and love. Amen.

For One's Teachers

Dear Jesus, You were the perfect Teacher when You were on earth. Help me to listen to and obey my teachers. When I am in school, my teachers take the place of my parents. My parents represent You, O God. Give my teachers help to do their hard work. Help me appreciate all their work and kindness for me. Amen.

For One's Priests

Thank You, God, for giving me parish priests to carry on Your work. Dear Jesus, the priest has an indelible but invisible mark of You, the High Priest, upon his soul. I must respect the priest because he has Your power to forgive sins and change bread and wine into Your Body and Blood. The priest is like another Christ.

Dear Jesus, even though priests take Your place, yet they are still men. Help them when they are lonely and when things get hard for them. I thank You, Jesus, for giving us priests who sacrifice their lives to adore You and to save souls. Bless all priests and especially my parish priests. Amen.

For One's School

Thank You, God, for giving me a school where I can learn many things about the world You have made. I want to be thankful for parents and all those who sacrifice to make my school possible. Dear God, I want to keep my school clean and everyone happy in my school. St. Thomas Aquinas, patron of Catholic schools, watch over my school that I may learn well the things of God and that many souls may come to God. Amen.

For Friends

Dear Jesus, thank You for giving me friends. I'll try to be a good example to my friends so that we all can love You and Your Blessed Mother better. Help me, dear Jesus, to be kind to my friends. Help me to share. Help me not to be mean but to be kind. I want to help others to be happy by being happy myself.

O guardian angel of mine, guide me so that I may always be fair with my friends. Speak to the guardian angels of my friends for me so that we all may be good and full of joy. Amen.

For a Sick Person

Jesus, I remember from the Bible that one time you made the sick mother-in-law of Peter suddenly well. You often cured the sick and the crippled. You loved sick people. I ask You, dear Jesus, by the power in Your holy Body and Soul, to make well the sick person for whom I now pray. Amen.

For the Souls of the Unborn

My Jesus, You are the Author of life. My Mother, Mary, you are the Mother of life. Jesus, when You were an infant, the Holy Innocents were murdered at Bethlehem because of You. Today, babies are being murdered even before they are born. All babies have souls, even before they come into the world. I ask You, dear Jesus, to touch people's hearts so that all babies may be born, see the light of day, and be baptized in saving waters.

Mary, pray for every child that every mother carries under her heart. You once carried the Child Jesus near your Immaculate Heart. Mary, through your prayers, lead all souls to heaven — especially those souls of the unborn — who have most need of mercy. Amen.

For the Hungry of the World

Kind and loving Father in heaven, You provide for the whole world. There are millions of people who are hungry. They don't have enough to eat. Feed their bodies and feed their souls.

Help us to turn from sin and share the good things of this earth with one another. Help us to teach others to help themselves. I know that You will always give the means to feed us, O God, if we only open our hearts and listen. Amen.

For the Poor

Lord, how You love poor people. You were poor Yourself, dear Jesus, when You were on earth. Your foster father, St. Joseph, was a poor carpenter. You lived in a poor home, and as You grew up You helped St. Joseph in his hard work to make a living.

You were God, dear Jesus. You could have had many things for Your Body and for the Holy Family that You did not have. You wanted to be rich only in Your Soul. And still, dear Jesus, You want people to have enough to eat, clothes to wear, and a place to live. When others do not have these things, You said that You suffer in them.

Dear Jesus, I want You, in Your poor people, to have things that are needed. I do not want You to lack clothes, food, or a home. I pray for the poor. I shall try always to share the things I have with others who have less. Amen.

For the Conversion of Sinners

O my God, You do not want the sinner to die in his sin. You want all people to come to You and to live with You forever. Jesus, You died on the Cross for everyone. Your saving death left no one out. You shed Your precious Blood for everyone. You redeemed the whole world. You are the Redeemer of all people.

But dear God, some people do not show their faith, their hope, or their love for You. Some people even dirty their souls with serious sin. They live apart from You. Your life does not fill their souls. If they die this way, they will not go to heaven. They will be lost in hell forever. I do not want that, O Jesus. You do not want that either.

Through the prayers of Mary, all the angels and saints, I join my own poor prayers, my Lord and my God, asking for the conversion of all sinners. Bring them to save their souls. Amen.

For the Conversion of a Parent

My dearest God in heaven, I know that You see all and hear all things. I am Your child. I thank You for bringing me to holy baptism. I thank You for giving me the gift of the one true faith. But now, my Lord and my God, I come before You to pray for this parent of mine who does not have the fullness of the one true faith.

It was no goodness of my own, dear God, that caused me to be baptized and to come to know the true faith. It was not the fault of my parent that he (she) was not brought up in the holy Catholic faith. You have given many good things to this parent of mine. He (she) has been willing to have me taught and to let me practice the holy Catholic faith. Now I ask You, dear God, to give the free gift of the faith to my parent. I ask You and I beg You to give the gift of that same faith You put into the hearts of the Apostles and first Christians when You started the Catholic Church almost two thousand years ago. I know that You hear all prayers. Hear this prayer of mine. Bring my parent even closer to You in faith and in love. Amen.

For the Conversion of Russia

Almighty God of heaven and earth, I beg You through the Sacred Heart of Jesus and the Immaculate Heart of Mary to convert Russia to the one true faith. Many people in Russia have long loved the Mother of God. Through her Immaculate Heart, bring peace to all peoples in Russia. Convert them to the fullness of true faith. Then spread Your love and true faith throughout all the world. I shall make sacrifices to bring this about.

Thank you, Jesus and Mary, for enabling Russia to give up the communistic and atheistic government of its land as the fruit of the Pope and bishops of the world consecrating the world and Russia to the Immaculate Heart of Mary on March 25, 1984. Amen.

For the Conversion of America

O Blessed Mother, America has been placed under your patronage and privilege of the Immaculate Conception. And yet, there is so much sin in America. At Guadalupe, in 1531, you appeared as the Immaculate Conception. You are imaged on St. Juan Diego's tilma as the Immaculate Conception and as the first Tabernacle of Jesus Christ, as you are there with child. Intercede through your Son, Jesus Christ, to stop the scourge of abortion and the culture of death in our land. Intercede so that Catholics everywhere develop greater love and faith for the Real Presence of your Son, Jesus Christ, in the Holy Eucharist.

O heavenly Mother Mary, intercede for the protection of the sanctity of marriage. Help all to know that God intends marriage to be permanent and only between one man and one woman.

Save our land from terrorists and hatreds of all kinds. Our country has drifted far from the fullness of true faith. Intercede, O holy Mother of the Church, that America be converted back to Jesus Christ, your Son, true God and true Man. Amen.

For the Conversion of Terrorists

Heavenly Father, we ask in the name of your Son, our Lord and Savior Jesus Christ, that terrorists be converted from using violence to using peaceful dialogue. May they realize that deliberate killing of human life and destruction of property is never in the plan of God to achieve justice and rights. Give wisdom to all to know that a war that deliberately kills innocent human lives can never be "holy."

Enable all people to live in purity and honesty of truth. May all come to know in faith that Jesus Christ is the Way, the Truth, and the Life.

Through the intercession of Mary, Mother of the Church, we ask that terrorists realize the error of their ways and come to the love and peace that only Jesus Christ can give. Amen.

For Refugees

Almighty God, You are the heavenly Father of all. All people on earth are Your children. You love everyone. See how some of Your children are suffering. Wars and persecutions, selfishness and hatred, drive people apart. Many good people, even little children, have been driven from their homes. Some have even had to leave their own country.

O Jesus, how You suffer today in refugees. How You suffer in those who do not have enough clothes or food or a home. Once, Jesus, You said of Yourself that You did not have a place whereon to lay Your head. It is still true today in Your brothers and sisters who have been driven from their homes.

Thank You, Jesus, for all You have given me. I ask that others not have to suffer. I shall try to bring love to others, for peace in the world must begin within me. Amen.

For the Clergy

Dear Jesus, I want to pray now especially for bishops, priests, and deacons. Through the Sacrament of Holy Orders, these men of God have the seal of You, Jesus, upon their souls in a very special way. The bishop can ordain other men, and he must show Your authority in the Church. The priest acts in Your Name to forgive sins and change bread and wine into Your own Body and Blood. The deacon can preach Your holy word and baptize new members into the Church.

O dear Jesus, what a great work You have given bishops, priests, and deacons. Thank You for giving to their souls Your own powers. Keep them pure and safe within Your holy Church. Do not let them become too sad or lonely when people do not listen to Your Church. Give them strength, and help them to remember that sometimes people did not listen to You either, and that they turned against You. I want to pray for Your special helpers, dear Jesus, because Your Church needs them always. Amen.

For Religious

Dear God of heaven, how much You must love Your religious — priests, brothers, and sisters. These men and women have given themselves entirely to You by vows of poverty, chastity, and obedience. They want to have nothing but You, dear Lord. They want always to be pure and holy, and to obey You and those who represent You.

Thank You, Jesus, for giving the Church religious men and women who glorify God and work to save souls. I pray that Your religious will always be true to the vows that they have taken, so as to love and serve God better. Amen.

For Seminarians

Lord Jesus Christ, Son of the Living God, You who promised that the heavenly Father will give the Holy Spirit to those who ask Him, I ask this of our heavenly Father in Your name for all seminarians, and especially for the seminarian I now pray for.

Grant a strong faith to each and every seminarian studying for the holy Catholic priesthood. Grant them loyalty to the teachings of Holy Mother Church and to the Pope, in a special way. I ask that they be formed in the likeness of Jesus Christ, open to the Holy Spirit, and become special sons of our heavenly Father.

CHRIST AND THE SEMINARIAN

Mary, Mother of God and Mother of the Church, as Our Lady of Vocations, intercede with your Divine Son for an increase in priestly vocations and to grant courage and perseverance to seminarians now studying and being formed in the likeness of Jesus Christ. Pray with us that laborers be sent into the vineyard of the Lord. Spouse of the Holy Spirit and first Daughter of the Father, keep our seminarians within the refuge of your Immaculate Heart.

St. Theresa, patroness of seminarians, through your prayers in heaven, plant the seeds of many vocations in the hearts of boys and young men. Make the seeds of vocations grow and bloom. Pray that the Church may have the blossoms of many vocations to the holy priesthood. Amen.

For the Rights of All People

My God, You created all people with a soul made in Your image and likeness. You created all people with souls that will live forever. You want us all to live upon this earth for a while and then live forever with You in heaven. You gave us all the right to life. You made us all free, and You wanted us to be able to find happiness.

My Lord and my God, all people have rights. None of us must ever take away the rights of others in order to enjoy ourselves more. That would be selfishness. That would not be just or right. That would be taking away rights that You gave to all.

Help me, God, to respect the rights of others and be willing to defend always what is just and what is right. Amen.

For Reparation for Sinners

Jesus, I wish to offer this prayer and sacrifice for people who sin in many ways. I wish to make reparation for those who eat too much. I wish to satisfy Your love for those who think bad thoughts or do bad things.

O heavenly Father, I wish to please the hearts of Jesus and Mary for the wounds they receive by sins of the eyes. I want to adore You, my God, at holy Mass for those who sin by not worshiping You through Mass every Sunday, the Lord's Day. Forgive people for their sins. Bring all to Your love. Amen.

For a Pure Heart

My Jesus, if I keep my thoughts clean, then I will have a pure heart. Dear Jesus, You know every thought that comes into my mind. I never want to offend You by deliberate bad thoughts.

My Lord and my God, if I think clean thoughts, I will speak good words and will do good things. You have said that where my heart is, there is my treasure. My Jesus, the only treasure I want for all eternity is to live in Your love and to have a soul that is like the Immaculate Heart of Your Mother. For this I ask. Amen.

For Purity

O Jesus, I want to be clean in my thoughts, words, and actions. I want always to think good thoughts. I want to speak good and holy words. In all I do, I will remember that the eyes of God always see me. Help me control my eyes.

O Immaculate Virgin, Mother of God, pray for me that my soul may be as spotless as the sweet host of your Son, Jesus, I receive in Holy Communion. O Immaculate Mary, you were never touched by the slightest sin. Keep my soul pure and holy. Pray for me that I may always live in the grace of Jesus, which is His life in me. St. Joseph, may I be as pure as fresh-blooming lilies through your powerful prayers. Amen.

For a Good Conscience

My loving God, I want always to form a good and correct conscience. O Holy Spirit, come into my soul. Give me Your light that I may know only what is true.

Holy Spirit, guide me in listening to the true teachings of the holy Catholic Church. The Church is guided by You to know rightly the word of God. I must listen to the Church, to the Pope and bishops. Jesus said to the Church, "He who hears you hears Me."

Jesus, help me to be true to You and to myself in living a good life. Amen.

For a Clean Tongue

My Jesus, I want to use my tongue only for what is good. Upon my tongue is placed the sacred host when I receive You in Holy Communion. The consecrated host is your Body, Blood, Soul, and Divinity. I want to use my tongue only to speak good things and to praise You, my God.

Dear God, You have said that when I am judged I will have to answer for every wrong word that my tongue spoke. Help me to use my tongue in such a way that when I am judged my guardian angel may announce that my tongue was used to glorify You, my God. Help all souls, and prepare my way to heaven. Amen.

For Those Dying

Many people will die this day, my Lord. Many are dying at this very moment, somewhere in the world. Bless them, O Jesus. Bring them to salvation. O Mother Mary, pray for their souls now that they are about to appear before God to be judged.

O heavenly Father, look at the sufferings that Your Son once had as He carried His Cross and hung upon it. Consider His holy thirst for the salvation of souls. Look, too, upon the great love of the Immaculate Heart of Mary. She once stood beneath the Cross and prayed for the conversion of sinners.

My Jesus, I now join my intentions to the holy Sacrifice of the Mass being offered around the world. From the power of the holy Mass, I ask You to give special graces to those who are now dying. Save them from the fires of hell, especially those who have most need of Your mercy. Amen.

For the Souls in Purgatory

Poor souls in purgatory, you are poor because you cannot help yourselves. But I can help you by my prayers and sacrifices, because the saints in heaven, you in purgatory, and the souls on earth make up the Communion of Saints. I wish to offer this prayer, and my prayers and sacrifices of this day, to lessen your sufferings and hurry the day of your entry into the glory of heaven.

Eternal rest grant unto them, O Lord, and let perpetual light shine upon them. May the souls of all the faithful departed, through the mercy of God, rest in peace. Amen.

For Religious Vocations

Dear God, touch the souls of many boys and girls so that they may hear Your call, to come follow Your Son, Jesus Christ. The harvest is indeed great, but the workers are few. I pray You, dear Lord of the harvest, to send a religious vocation to many young people so that they may serve You all the days of their life in the special work of the Church. Amen.

For Priestly Vocations

Dear Jesus, You need many more priests to do Your work in the Church. The Church can exist only if it has priests to forgive sins in Your Name and to perpetuate the holy Sacrifice of the Cross, which is the Mass. You need priests to preach Your holy word and to bind up the wounds of souls hurt and separated from God.

Dear Jesus, I believe that the greatest vocation on earth to which You can call anyone is to be Your priest forever. I come to ask You to call many boys and young men to follow You, the High Priest. Give them courage to make the necessary sacrifices. Give them hearts to love You generously and with which to love souls for Your sake, my Lord. May many hear Your call, "Come, follow Me." Amen.

For a Good Harvest

Lord of the harvest, You want to feed both bodies and souls. Give good crops to our farmers. Bring the right amount of rain and sunshine. As You warm our fields for growth, warm our hearts for loving You and our neighbors.

There are many hungry people in the world, dear God. They need food. Our farmers provide the needed food. But, dear God, only You can bless the work of our farmers so that our fields bring forth good things for food and clothing and shelter.

As a good Father, dear God, I trust that You will give Your people the things they need. Thank You. Amen.

To Love Everyone

My Lord and my God, I want to love everyone. You love everyone. You loved everyone so much that You died for us all in Your Son, Jesus Christ.

When I do not love others, it is because I wrongly think I am better than they are. But, dear God, whatever is good in me came from You. There is goodness in everyone. Help me to see Your goodness in everyone.

Everyone is made in Your image and likeness, my God. I will love everyone I meet, and even those I do not meet. I will think, "I love everyone, because God loves everyone." Amen.

To Share

My Jesus, help me to share the good things You have given me. I must not be selfish. I must share with those who have less and are in real need.

Dear God, help me to share my things with those who will use them well. When others share with me, help me to respect what is not mine and to be thankful. All good things come from You, God, and all the children I know are Your children, too. Amen.

To Know Oneself

Help me, my God, to know myself in Your Son, Jesus Christ. You have placed me in this world at this particular time. You had a purpose in making me. I want to give my life to loving You, dear God. I want to leave the world a little better because You placed me in it.

All-knowing and all-loving Father of heaven, You have given me certain gifts and talents. Help me to discover them. Help me to develop and use them to the best of my ability. May I never use Your gifts except in humility and thankfulness and for Your glory. Amen.

To Be True to Oneself

Jesus, You are Truth itself. I want to be true to myself. When I place myself in You and find myself in You, my Jesus, then I am true to myself. I want to follow You, dear Jesus, who said, "I am the Way, the Truth, and the Life." Help me not to pretend I am something or someone other than I am. You made me, O God, because You love me with an everlasting love. Had You wanted me to be other than I am, You would have made me that way. Help me to be satisfied.

Dear God, whatever talents, whatever gifts, You have given me, I will try to use them. I will be happy in You, dear Jesus. I will try to do my best each day. In being happy each day, knowing and loving You in all I meet, I can be true to myself, dear Lord. I want to be true to You, Jesus. In You I live, move, and have my being. Amen.

To Mary to Love Jesus

Immaculate Mary, you are my Mother and model in loving Jesus. No one ever loved Jesus more than you or as greatly as you do. You were the perfect woman of faith on earth. You are the model of all that the Church should be. And you loved Jesus so much. Your Immaculate Heart offered Jesus in sacrifice upon the Cross. You laid down your Son in sacrifice of reparation as He hung dying on the Cross.

It was not easy for you to love Jesus and to love the entire Blessed Trinity so much, my Mother. Your heart always beat as one with the heart of Jesus. When Jesus willed to offer His life on the Cross, with a greater love than anyone else could have, sweet heart of Mary, you made the same offering. How you wished you could have died in His place. You felt the pain in your heart.

Mary, my Mother, your Immaculate Heart is most like Jesus' Sacred Heart. Make my heart like yours in loving Jesus. Amen.

To Jesus to Love Mary

Jesus, my Lord and my God, I want You to help me to love Mary the way I should. No one loved our Blessed Lady more than You did. You were her perfect Son. You made Mary the most beautiful and the greatest of all women. You made Mary so great because You made her to be Your Mother. Jesus, You loved Mary more than all the angels and saints taken together.

Jesus, You are my perfect Model, and the Model for all people in loving Mary. We imitate You, dear Jesus, when we love Your Mother. We can never love Your most holy Mother enough or as much as You do. Still, dear Jesus, You can give each one of us the grace we need to love the heavenly Queen the way we should. Thank You for sharing Your Mother. Amen.

To Go to Heaven

Dear God, I want to go to heaven some day. I want Jesus to save my soul. I want Mary to obtain for me, from her Son, all the graces I need for salvation.

Heaven is my true home for which You made me, O God. I will gladly spend what years You want of me on earth. Then I beg You to take me home to heaven, where I will see You face-to-face as You really are. I shall be so happy to be with Mary, Joseph, the saints, my guardian angel, and all the angels in heaven. Amen.

To Be Always Honest

Jesus, You said, "I am the Truth." You are the Way, the Truth, and the Life. Help me to be honest in all I do and say. I am made in the image and likeness of the Blessed Trinity. God, You gave me a soul that will live forever. When I am always honest and truthful, then I am truly living in Your image and likeness. Amen.

To Be Obedient

Almighty God, I am Your child. You have authority over me. You have placed a share of Your authority over me in others. First among them are my parents. My teachers also share Your authority. Everyone in authority has it from You. My priest, bishop, and our Pope represent You, Jesus. I want to obey Your authority, dear God.

The Bible tells me that when Jesus was twelve years old He went back home with Mary and Joseph and grew up obeying them. I ask You, O Child Jesus, to give me strength always to be obedient. Amen.

To Control One's Temper

Sometimes, dear Lord, I want my way only. I am tempted to give in to selfishness. Others get in my way. Then I am tempted to lose my temper. I must learn to control myself. By Your grace, O God, strengthen my weak will.

Jesus, even when You were falsely accused, You kept silent. You never complained. By Your sufferings, give me grace always to control my emotions. Amen.

To Be Generous

Thank You, dear God, for all the things that You have given me. I have food, clothing, and a home. You have given me health, a mind, and free will. Best of all, dear God, You have given me the gift of true faith. Help me to give in return.

Dear God, I want to give to others who have less. Now, when I am still young, I must learn to support, however small my means, Your Church, missionaries, and those who are hungry. Help me to share with others the love You give to me. Amen.

To Give Good Example

Jesus, I want to imitate You by always giving good example. Sometimes I fail. Sometimes I've been sulky and have not cooperated. But I want to show others how happy I am as a Catholic Christian. I must always be honest. I must never use wrong words.

Jesus, You became a child and were a boy in all things except sin. I know that You brought joy to others. You were an example to others in loving our heavenly Father. I must show my Christian love by helping and playing with the child who is lonely. Then, dear Jesus, it is the same as doing good things to You. Amen.

In Time of Temptation

Jesus, I do not want to offend You by sin. Your Sacred Heart is already too much offended. I think of the thorns pounded into Your head. I think of the big nails in Your hands and feet. I think, too, of the whips that tore into Your sacred Body. I know, Jesus, that a temptation is not a sin. A temptation is a time for me to prove my love for You by not sinning.

How happy I am to know, Jesus, that You promised that You will never permit me to be tempted too strongly. You will always give me grace to overcome every temptation. I am weak, Jesus. In You, dear Jesus, I am strong. Amen.

To Grow in Faith

I believe, Lord — help my unbelief. Make me strong in faith. I cannot come to You, O Jesus, unless the power of the Holy Spirit comes upon me. This I want. I cannot come to God the Father except through You, O Jesus. This is my desire. I want to believe, to adore, to trust, and to love You, O God.

My God, I believe in You. I would rather die than deny You. Make my faith strong. I beg pardon for those who do not believe. Grant them faith. Amen.

To Accept Criticism

Sacred Heart of Jesus, help me to accept criticism. May I humbly see the truth when others point out my mistakes to me. May I use such criticism to change my ways so as to make my heart more like Yours through Your grace.

Jesus, when I am criticized wrongly, help me then, too, to be humble and remember when You were falsely accused. You offered it up in reparation for the sins of the world. Whatever sufferings come my way through false criticism I shall offer up for love of You, Jesus, and for the conversion of sinners. Amen.

To Be Silent

St. Joseph, husband of the Virgin Mother, Mary, and foster father of Jesus Christ, the Bible does not record a single word you ever spoke. God's word says that you were a just man. How you loved silence, so as to do your work and show your love for Jesus and Mary. St. Joseph, pray that I may learn how to listen and how to observe silence.

Almighty Father in heaven, there is so much noise upon earth. Help me to spend some time each day in silence so that I can hear You speaking to me about the love You have for me in Your Son, Jesus Christ. In silence, I want often to remember that the Most Blessed Trinity lives in my soul by grace. Speak, Lord, Your child is listening. Amen.

To Be Humble

Jesus, meek and humble of heart, make my heart like Yours. Mary, the most humble of all persons after Jesus, I ask your prayers that I may not brag, but instead give all credit to God. Immaculate Heart of Mary, you prayed, "He who is mighty has done great things for me." If I accomplish anything, I must always give the credit to God.

Jesus, help me never to look down on others. Help me also not to be jealous of those who have greater gifts than I have. Help me to do the best with what I have been given and to be happy in Your love. Amen.

To Know One's Vocation

Lord, what will You have me do? Send forth Your Spirit into my heart so that I may know what Your will is for me. I know, dear God, that I will find happiness only in doing Your will. By doing Your will, I will serve You, my God, and love my neighbor. Speak to me, Lord, as I listen to learn Your will. Amen.

To Hear God's Word

My Jesus, You are the Word of God made flesh. You are God the Son, and You came to earth from

God the Father to teach us the way and to redeem us from sin. Men put You to death. Of some You had to say, "Having ears, they hear not; having eyes, they see not."

O dear Jesus, help me to hear Your word with the ears of my soul, and to see You clearly with spiritual eyes. Send the Holy Spirit into my soul so that when I hear Your holy word spoken in Church, in religious instructions, and at home, I may clearly know that You, my loving Jesus, are speaking. Speak, Lord, Your servant listens. Amen.

To Keep the Word of God

Jesus Christ, Word of God made flesh, I want to keep Your holy word by living it. I take for my model the Blessed Virgin Mary, Your Mother. Your heavenly Mother and my heavenly Mother kept the word of God in her Immaculate Heart. She thought often on the mysteries of Your life, dear Jesus.

O heavenly Queen of mine, you who conceived Jesus in your Immaculate Heart, even before you conceived Him in your precious womb, pray that I may always remember to know and love the word of God and to live it. Pray to the Holy Spirit, who overshadowed you, to come to me, to help me keep God's holy word. Amen.

To Avoid Waste

O dear heavenly Father, You have given me all that I need. I have food, clothing, and a good home. Help me not to waste food. Help me not to throw good food away when many children in the world are hungry and even starving. Dear God, help me to take care of my clothes and respect the property in my home.

Thank You, dear God, for giving me so many things. I never want to waste the gifts You give me. Amen.

To Thank God for Grace

O my loving God, how happy I am to be in Your grace. By grace I share in Your own life. I share in Your nature as God. By baptism I was first made Your child, O God. By prayers and good works, and especially by holy Mass and Holy Communion, I grow in Your life within me.

Dear God, I am not worthy of such greatness. You who are mighty have given me a share in Your own love. By grace I can know and love You. By sharing in Your life within my soul on earth, I shall be led to eternal life with You, my God, in heaven. Thank You. Amen.

To Grow in Grace

My God, You came to this earth as Jesus Christ, to give Your life to us. You wanted to give Your life to souls more generously. That is why You became Man in Jesus Christ.

Dear Jesus, the Author of life and the Source of all grace, I come to ask You to increase Your divine life within me. Make me love You more and more.

Help me to serve You more generously. Increase my faith, my hope. I want to open my heart and my soul by prayer, by good works, and by receiving the holy Sacraments of your Church so that You can fill me with Your grace. Amen.

To Bless One's Home

Most Blessed Trinity — Father, Son, and Holy Spirit — send down Your blessings on all who live in this house.

Protect my home from storms and fire and all kinds of danger. Keep us from sin. Keep us in Your love.

Holy Immaculate Mother of God and glorious St. Joseph, protectors and patrons of our homes, save and protect us now and at the hour of our death. Amen.

PRAYERS TO GOD

To the Holy Spirit to Know the Truth

Come, Holy Spirit, Spirit of Truth. There is so much confusion in the world. People say different things. Some say, "This is true" or "That is true." But dear Jesus, I know that You alone are Truth itself. It was You, my Lord, who said, "I am the Truth."

Jesus, You promised the Holy Spirit to keep Your holy, catholic, and apostolic Church always in the truth. You said that You would be with it until the end of the world. When people say different things,

I will call upon the Holy Spirit, as I do now, to keep me loyal to Your true Church. I shall always listen to and obey the Pope, who is the visible head of the Church on earth. Amen.

To the Child Jesus

My Jesus, when You lived on earth, You were once my age. How deeply and perfectly You loved Your heavenly Father. While on earth You always obeyed Your parents — Mary and Joseph.

I know, my Jesus, that now that You are in heaven, You are the very same Jesus who was born of Mary, who helped St. Joseph in his carpenter shop when You were a boy, and who at the age of twelve surprised the doctors in the Temple by Your great wisdom and answers. You, whom I receive in Holy Communion, are the same Jesus who rose from the dead and ascended into heaven.

My Jesus, You understand children, for You Yourself were once a little child. You love God's children so much that You became one of us. By the love and grace that were Yours when You were the same age that I now am, I ask, dear Jesus, that You make me grow in knowledge, love, and grace. Amen.

To Jesus, Who Has Died, Is Risen, and Will Come Again

Jesus, You have died for me. You are risen for me. You will come again for me. You died for all people, but You thought of me, too, dear Jesus, when You suffered so much. You thought of my sins. You thought of Your love for me.

Jesus, You are risen. That You rose from the dead proves that You are God as well as Man. This is how I know that my faith in You, Jesus, is good and true. You are my Savior because You died, and You are my God because You are risen.

Jesus, You will come again. At the end of the world, You will return to this earth. The dead will rise from their graves. We will all get our bodies back from the dust. Then all the people who have lived on this earth, believed in You, loved You, and died in Your grace will go to heaven with You, their bodies and souls united forever.

Yes, dear Jesus, I believe in the resurrection of the body. I believe that You will come again and judge all people. Amen.

To Jesus Crucified

My Jesus, how You suffered on the Cross for me and for everyone else in the world. For three long hours You hung dying on the Cross. Your dearest friends had deserted You. They ran away and hid. Only John, a few holy women, and Your dear Mother remained at the foot of the Cross. These showed You love and respect. The others made fun of You. They insulted You, spat at You, and hurt You.

I can still see, dear Jesus, the thorns that cruel men pounded into Your holy head. They cover Your head, and every movement of Your head causes the thorns to hurt You more. The big nails in Your feet and wrists cause so much pain, as You lose more and more of Your all-holy and all-precious Blood. The whip marks from the beating at the pillar hurt You from head to toe. And You are thirsty, Jesus. You are thirsty for souls. You are suffering for me. You are suffering for the whole world. O Jesus, how much You loved us. You loved the world so much that You died on the Cross.

I adore You, O Christ, and I bless You, because by Your holy Cross You have redeemed the world. Amen.

To the God of All Colors

O God of many colors, how beautiful You made this world. The trees, the sky, the water, the clouds, the grass, the mountains, the prairies — all things reflect in some small way the perfect beauty that is Yours, my God.

And dear God, You made people different colors, too. Some are black. Others are brown, yellow, red, or white. You live in all people. You love all people. I am happy that You made us beautiful but different, and that You made every one of us in Your own image and likeness. Thank You, God, for all colors. Amen.

PRAYERS TO SAINTS

The Holy Family

Jesus, Mary, and Joseph, you were the perfect family. The world has you three as the perfect model and example of Christian family love. You helped one another while on earth. Now from heaven you help all families.

Jesus, You obeyed Mary and Joseph. The Bible says so. The word of God says that at the age of twelve, You went back home and grew up obeying Your parents. Help me to obey my parents. Jesus, Mary, and Joseph, I give you my heart and my soul. I love you. Amen.

Blessed Jacinta and Blessed Francisco

Blessed Jacinta of Fátima, help me to live a life of prayer and sacrifice for sinners as you did. Help me to love the Immaculate Heart of Mary as you did and to work to save souls from hell.

ICON OF BLESSED FRANCISCO AND BLESSED JACINTA

Blessed Francisco of Fátima, pray that I, like you, will think often of God and console Him who is so sad because He is offended by sin. Obtain for me a strong will to walk away from bad companions as you did.

Blessed Jacinta and Blessed Francisco, help me to pray the Rosary often as both of you did. Help me to pray the Rosary properly while thinking of the mysteries of Jesus and Mary. Ask my guardian angel to lead me to adore the hidden Jesus in the Most Blessed Sacrament, just as the angel of Fátima led you to Jesus. Pray that I offer the Body, Blood, Soul, and Divinity of Jesus Christ to the Blessed Trinity, as you did.

Blessed Jacinta and Blessed Francisco, pray that I be pure in thought, word, and deed, as you were. As you are the youngest children the Church has ever declared "Blessed," pray that I, too, will someday live in heaven with you. Amen.

Guardian Angel
(Traditional)

Angel of God, my guardian dear, to whom God's love commits me here; ever this day be at my side, to light and guard, to rule and guide. Amen.

All Guardian Angels

Guardian angels, you who have been given the work by God to watch over people on earth, I come to you now. May you, too, pray that I love and be kind to the people I meet for whom you care. Help me to meet people with whom I can work to adore God better and bring souls to Jesus. Talk to my own guardian angel that he may move me to be loving and kind, and to respond in goodness to the people for whom you care. Amen.

All Angels

Angels of God in heaven, you who are arranged in nine choirs before God, I come to ask your prayers. God has made each one of you with a great intellect and with great power. You are persons, spirits without bodies. Before God you always use your free wills to love God and do His holy will. O angels of God, take my message of love to almighty God. Adore for me Jesus Christ, your King and my King. Give my love to Mary, your heavenly Queen and my Queen. Bow down before the Most Blessed Trinity and ask for peace for the world.

Angels of God, I look forward to the day when I shall join you in heaven. Pray for me, for my family, for my friends, for holy Mother Church on earth, for everyone. Amen.

St. Michael the Archangel

St. Michael the Archangel, defend us in battle; be our defense against the wickedness and snares of the devil. May God rebuke him, we humbly pray; and do you, O prince of the heavenly host, by the power

ST. MICHAEL THE ARCHANGEL

of God, thrust into hell Satan and the other evil spirits who prowl about the world for the ruin of souls. Amen.

V. Most Sacred Heart of Jesus.
R. Have mercy on us *(three times).*

All Saints

Saints of heaven, I ask your prayers. I know that there are millions of you in heaven. You once lived on earth. Now you see God face-to-face in all His beauty and goodness. On earth you were like ordinary people. But in your hearts and souls you had faith, love, and grace from Jesus, which brought you to heaven.

All the saints in heaven, remember us still here on earth. Pray for us, as we are part of the same Communion of Saints. Amen.

Patron Saint

Good St. _____, thank you for being my special protector in heaven. How happy I am to have the same name you had when you lived on earth. Now you see God face-to-face. How beautiful God must be! Talk to God about me. Tell Him I love Him. And His Mother, too — tell Mary how I love her Immaculate Heart.

My dear patron saint, I want to imitate the good virtues you had. Help me to live so as to adore God and help others to heaven. I want to be a saint in heaven someday, too. Pray for me now and always. Amen.

St. Joseph

Good St. Joseph, husband of the Mother of God, I come to ask you to watch over me and everyone in the holy Church of Jesus Christ. St. Joseph, you are the greatest of all the saints in heaven after Mary and Jesus. God chose you to be the foster father of His Son, Jesus Christ. Of all men, you were the most just, the most holy, the most worthy to take care of the Holy Family.

I want to follow your good example, St. Joseph, in learning to keep silent when I should. I want to be one who loves Jesus and Mary as you did. I want to die a holy and happy death, as you did, in the arms of Jesus and Mary. Good St. Joseph, pray for me. Amen.

St. Joseph
(By Blessed Pope John XXIII)

St. Joseph, guardian of Jesus and chaste spouse of Mary, you passed your life in perfect fulfillment of duty. You supported the Holy Family of Nazareth with the work of your hands. Kindly protect those who trustingly turn to you. You know their aspirations, their hardships, their hopes; and they turn to you because they know you will understand and protect them. You, too, have known trial, labor, and weariness. But even amid the worries of material life, your soul was filled with deep peace and sang out in true joy through intimacy with the Son of God entrusted to you, and with Mary, His tender Mother. Amen.

The St. Joseph Promise

St. Joseph, spouse of the Mother of God, head of the Holy Family and guardian of virgins, to you I give my promise of virginity. I will live a life of virginity until I have received the blessings of the Sacrament of Holy Matrimony.

I promise to live the ideals of the Sixth and Ninth Commandments by decency in word, action, and dress, and in the use of the media. When necessary I will let others know where I stand in such matters, in the hope of leading them to greater purity of life.

I will work to maintain this promise by the frequent use of sacramental confession and by cultivating a strong personal devotion to the Sacred Heart of Jesus and to the Immaculate Heart of Mary.

St. Joseph, protector of the Holy Church, in union with Mary, Mother of the Church, and my guardian angel, present to the Blessed Trinity my promise of virginity and my pledge to live the virtue of holy purity. Amen.

I commit myself to keeping the St. Joseph Promise as it appears above.

_____

(Signature)

St. Thomas More
("The Merry Saint")

St. Thomas More, the merry saint, pray that I may imitate your Christian merriness. May I also respect human life as you did. Whenever a new baby was about to be born into this world, you would keep praying until you learned it had arrived happily into the light of this world.

Good St. Thomas, how you loved your country and your Church. You had the greatest love for family life, and for holy marriage as well. You went to your death to defend the holiness of marriage. You went to your death to defend the Pope as the chief authority of Jesus on earth. Pray, St. Thomas More, that all people today may love life, love their country and the Church, and be obedient to the Pope as you were. Amen.

St. Philip Neri

May I be a lay apostle of joy, purity, and true teachings as you were, St. Philip Neri, for so many years. May I be open to the Holy Spirit as you were when the Holy Spirit came to you as a ball of fire in the catacomb of St. Sebastian.

When you finally accepted the call to the holy priesthood, St. Philip, even though you considered yourself not worthy, you worked hard to help souls in the confessional and to teach the true faith. Help me always to appreciate the Sacraments of Penance and the Holy Eucharist. Amen.

St. Clare
(Patroness of Television)

St. Clare, you who were led to be a bride of Christ through the preaching of St. Francis of Assisi, pray that I, too, will never be attached to the things of the world. Help me to look only to the joys of heaven and to use the things of this world as step-ping-stones to my true and eternal home.

You loved the holy Sacrifice of the Mass so much, St. Clare, that God permitted you to see the Mass offered on Christmas Eve even at a distance. Now that you are the patroness of television, give me the strength to watch only what is good for the soul. Amen.

St. Tarcisius

St. Tarcisius, youthful martyr of the Holy Eucharist, give me through your heavenly prayers such a love for Jesus in the Blessed Sacrament that I would be willing to die for Him.

Pray that I may always receive Jesus in Holy Communion with a pure heart. Pray that I will adore the Real Presence of Jesus and always act reverently in church. Amen.

St. Elizabeth Ann Seton

St. Elizabeth Ann, chosen to be the first native-born American saint, pray for me and all Americans. As you came to the one true faith when an adult, may I always remain true to the holy Catholic Church, which Jesus founded.

Pray for our Catholic schools. Pray for all children to grow in the knowledge of true faith. Pray for unity among all Christians. May I share the great love you had for Jesus in the Most Blessed Sacrament. Amen.

St. Bernadette

St. Bernadette, you to whom Our Lady appeared when you were fourteen years old and said, "I am the Immaculate Conception," now that you are in heavenly glory, pray that we may come to the knowledge and love of God's Mother that heaven gave to you.

May we remember the words you called out when Mary was appearing to you: "Penitence! Penitence! Penitence!" And another time, "Pray, pray, pray for poor sinners."

O favored St. Bernadette, your body, though long dead, refuses to turn to dust and remains fresh as if sleeping. Keep us mindful that we are meant for heaven, and our bodies for resurrection. Amen.

St. Martin de Porres

St. Martin de Porres, you whom God favored with black skin and a love for all peoples — especially the poor — pray that we may look upon everyone with love.

Pray that we may always keep our souls clean and pure, and realize that all races of the world belong to the one family of God. Amen.

St. Juan Diego
(In honor of the saint)

O Mother of mercy, as you appeared to St. Juan Diego some four hundred years ago near Mexico City and left your picture upon his humble cloak, we beg you to let his example serve to inspire us to be lay apostles. As once you chose St. Juan Diego as your instrument of grace in leading millions to God's priests for baptism, so now use us to guide and help our priests in the salvation of souls.

O ever-Virgin Mary of Guadalupe, you who are the entirely perfect Virgin, holy Mary, who by means of your image of Guadalupe crush the serpent, and through your Immaculate Heart shed graces of mercy on souls, always look upon us with a merciful glance.

Mirror our image in your eyes and in your Immaculate Heart, as you once reflected St. Juan Diego in your eyes when you miraculously appeared to him on the hill at Tepeyac. Amen.

St. John Vianney

St. John Vianney, patron of parish priests all over the world, I ask you to pray in heaven for many priestly vocations. Obtain from the Sacred Heart of Jesus, together with your intercession to the Immaculate Heart of Mary, that many boys and young men will hear the call of a priestly vocation. Obtain for them the generosity to answer "yes" and be willing to sacrifice themselves for God's glory and for the salvation of souls.

May all priests imitate you, St. John Vianney, in caring for souls in the confessional and in teaching young people the fullness of true faith. Amen.

St. Maximilian Mary Kolbe

O St. Maximilian Mary Kolbe, faithful follower of St. Francis of Assisi, inflamed by the love of God, you dedicated your life to works for the salvation of souls. You offered your life to save that of a fellow prisoner by saying, "I am a Catholic priest."

Having consecrated yourself to the Immaculate Virgin Mary, you inspire countless souls to a holy life of service, dedicated to Mary's Immaculate Heart and to a life of purity, and even martyrdom if necessary. Obtain for me the virtues of Christ that you lived so well on earth. Amen.

Blessed Kateri Tekakwitha
(In honor of the blessed)

Almighty God, You who favored Blessed Kateri with such purity that she is now called "Lily of the Mohawks" and the "Indian Little Flower," grant us the grace to be inspired by her life.

May we be inspired by Blessed Kateri's life to live a life of penance. May we practice reparation in the presence of the Blessed Sacrament and pray the Rosary with devotion such as this favored Indian girl did. Amen.

St. Joan of Arc

St. Joan of Arc, you who were inspired by angels, especially St. Michael the Archangel, to do God's will, pray from your heavenly place that I, too, may be loyal to both God and my country.

Pray that I will work to make things in life Christ-like. May my faith be strong that, like you, I would rather die than deny the truth. Amen.

St. Dominic Savio

St. Dominic Savio, you left this world when you were only fifteen years old. But you came close to God in your short time upon earth. You started serving the holy Sacrifice of the Mass when you were only six years old. Oh, how you loved the Holy Mass and to receive Jesus in Holy Communion. St. Dominic, I find so many things in your life that show me how to live a good Catholic life.

St. Dominic, for your motto you chose "Death, rather than sin." You went to confession to St. John Bosco every week so that you could be helped and understand how to do God's will better. You loved to help the priest and do whatever you could for souls. You even got other boys to make good confessions and give up bad things.

Just before you died, you said, "Father, what I can see is so beautiful." Now that you are in heaven, St. Dominic Savio, pray that I, too, may live a good Catholic life and be with God forever. Amen.

St. Aloysius Gonzaga
(Patron of Catholic Youth)

St. Aloysius Gonzaga, when you were on earth you trained to be a soldier. You kept away from bad companions. You learned to love God so much that you became a soldier for God rather than one who used a sword. You desired only to use the sword of God's holy word.

St. Aloysius, you who cared for the sick and risked your life in charity to take care of others, pray that I may always be well in body and in soul. You died as a young man with the Name of Jesus on your lips and your eyes on the Crucifix. Pray that I may ever keep the holy Name of Jesus on my lips and the grace of Jesus in my soul. Amen.

St. Louis de Montfort

Good St. Louis de Montfort, I thank you for teaching the world the meaning of consecration to Mary and true devotion to God's Mother.

Please pray to the holy Mother of God, St. Louis, that we may always understand correctly the way to Jesus through Mary. Amen.

St. John Bosco
(Patron of Youth)

St. John Bosco, great friend of boys and girls when you were on earth, be our friend still, now that you are in heaven. You were so kind and loving toward all young people. Look down upon me now as I ask for your very special prayers before the throne of God.

Help me to be a happy saint, just as you were always so happy. Pray that I may be happy in this life and then happy with God forever in heaven.

St. John Bosco, I want to have a holy joy, to be kind, to be good, to be meek and humble, as you were in imitation of Jesus Christ. I want to remember to thank God and people for all the favors I receive.

Thank you, St. John, for teaching us how to live the life of Jesus. Amen.

St. Maria Goretti

St. Maria Goretti, pray in heaven that I may love purity so much that I would be willing to die as you did, if necessary. I wish to keep my soul good and holy, as when it came from the waters of baptism and after my First Holy Communion. Your parish priest taught you, St. Maria, that you should be willing to die rather than ever commit a mortal sin. Thank you for showing young people that purity of soul is even more precious than a long life here on earth.

St. Maria Goretti, from your place in heaven, pray that I may be always pure and holy. Pray that all young people may be heroes in our fight against the evil spirit of wickedness. Amen.

St. Dominic

St. Dominic, by your prayers, I beg for the love of true teachings in my holy faith. Also, I want to share your love for the holy Rosary. From your place in heaven, St. Dominic, rekindle the flame of faith in those parts of the world that are now cold again to Jesus and Mary. Amen.

St. Theresa of the Child Jesus

St. Theresa, you who are called the "Little Flower," pray that I may always live as a good child of God. May I always do the little things of life extra well for the love of God. St. Theresa, you loved flowers and you wanted to give to Jesus the flowers of many, many souls.

Now that you are in heaven, let fall upon earth a shower of roses by your prayers. Bring many more souls to Jesus. Pray to the Mother of God for us that she will smile on her children here on earth. Amen.

St. Anthony Mary Claret

St. Anthony Mary Claret, pray that I may share the great love that you had for the Immaculate Heart of Mary. You loved Jesus so much in the Most Blessed Sacrament that Our Lord remained within you from one Holy Communion until the next.

St. Anthony, pray that I may have a loyalty to the Pope, as you had. At the First Vatican Council, it was you who so strongly defended the teaching that the Pope keeps the Church in truth on faith and morals.

Pray that I may love true teachings and live by true faith. May I express my true faith in love for the Immaculate Heart of Mary, who will lead me, like you, St. Anthony, to the hidden Jesus of the Holy Eucharist. Amen.

St. Margaret Mary Alacoque

O St. Margaret Mary Alacoque, you were especially loved by the Sacred Heart of Jesus. When you were praying before Jesus in the Most Blessed Sacrament of the Altar, He came out of the monstrance and showed you His holy heart burning with love for all people.

St. Margaret, the Sacred Heart of Jesus showed you His heart surrounded by thorns with which sinful men pierce it by their sins. Jesus was sad and in pain because many persons do not love Him.

Great saint of the Sacred Heart, pray that I may give back to Jesus the love He has for me and all persons. Help me to make reparation to Jesus in the Most Blessed Sacrament. May I learn to be full of thanks to Jesus for His love and for giving Himself to me in the Sacrament of Love. Amen.

PROMISES OF THE SACRED HEART OF JESUS TO ST. MARGARET MARY ALACOQUE

To lovers of the Sacred Heart:

- I will give them all graces necessary for their state of life.
- I will establish peace in their families.
- I will console them in all their pains and trials.
- I will be their assured refuge in life, and especially in death.

- I will shed abundant blessings upon all their undertakings.
- Sinners shall find in My heart an infinite ocean of mercy; and lukewarm souls shall be rendered fervent.
- Fervent souls shall rise rapidly to greater perfection.
- I will bless those houses where the image of My heart shall be exposed and honored.
- I will give to priests the gift of moving the hardest hearts.
- Persons who propagate [make known] this devotion shall have their names inscribed on My heart, never to be effaced from it.

(The Sacred Heart of Jesus, according to St. Margaret Mary Alacoque, asked that we receive Our Lord in Holy Communion on First Fridays in reparation for the sins committed against Him. Many Catholics piously believe that if this is done for at least nine continuous First Fridays, Jesus will see that they die in the state of grace necessary for salvation. One must, of course, plan to continue living a good Catholic life and be sincere.)

St. Anne

Holy St. Anne, how honored you were to be chosen by God to become the mother of the Blessed Virgin Mary. St. Anne, you are the mother of the

Mother of God. You are the grandmother of Jesus, the Son of God.

Pray for us, St. Anne, that we may honor and love God's Mother as you did. Pray for us to know the Mother of Jesus, who is the mediatrix of all graces. Mary was formed in your body and created in her soul without original sin. How holy you are, St. Anne, to have had such great things happen in you. Pray for us always. Amen.

St. Joachim

Holy St. Joachim, father of the Blessed Virgin Mary, your very name means "preparation of the Lord." By becoming the father of the Mother of God, you prepared the temple of the Lord. Mary's holy body became a tabernacle for Jesus, our Lord and Savior.

St. Joachim, you were chosen among all men to become the father of the Mother of Jesus Christ. Your daughter was made by God without original sin. Your daughter is the Immaculate Conception. How powerful your prayers are with God. Pray for my own father, St. Joachim, and pray for me. Amen.

St. Nicholas

Holy St. Nicholas, God has glorified you by many miracles. God gave you special power over flames. Pray for us that we may never be touched by the fires of hell.

St. Nicholas, you were known to give gifts to others. Through your prayers, bring to us the gift of God's grace. Teach us by your example to be generous to others. Amen.

St. Valentine

St. Valentine, you who inspire us to love God and one another in Christ, pray from your home in heaven that we may always live in Christian love.

St. Valentine, you were a holy priest on earth, and now that you are in heaven you still have the indelible mark of Christ's priesthood on your soul. You loved God so much that you became a martyr of love. May I love God and neighbor so much that I would be willing, if necessary, to lay down my life for my friends. Amen.

St. Peter

St. Peter, you are the Rock upon which Jesus built His holy Church. Pray for the Church on earth now that another Pope is the visible head of the Church. Jesus made you the first Pope and gave you the keys of the kingdom of heaven. Since then, Popes have had the power to bind and loose.

May I always respect the authority of the Pope, who speaks for Jesus. Pray, St. Peter, that all men may obey the authority which Jesus gave to you and which our Pope has today. St. Peter, I can know that where you are in your successor, the Pope, there is the Church. There, too, is Jesus Christ. Pray for me. Amen.

St. Francis of Assisi

Holy St. Francis of Assisi, pray for the Church on earth that you loved so much. Our Lord called you to build up the Church here on earth so that people would be strong in faith and love. Now that you are in heaven, pray that we may grow in faith and love.

St. Francis, you loved poverty and were not attached to worldly things. Help me to know that the things of earth are not what count, but rather the things of the spirit, which will lead me to heaven.

You loved our Lord Jesus Christ so much, St. Francis, that you had on your body the marks of the wounds of Jesus. Through your example and prayers, may I, too, come to live like Jesus and to die in His holy love. Amen.

St. Thomas Aquinas
(Patron of Catholic Schools)

St. Thomas Aquinas, may I be holy and pure, as you were. May I learn to study to the best of my power, as you did. May I be a lover of God's holy word in the Bible and be loyal to the holy Catholic Church in imitation of you who followed Jesus Christ so closely.

Watch over my school, St. Thomas. Help me and all students in my school to come to know and love God. Amen.

St. Faustina

St. Faustina, Apostle of Divine Mercy, thank you for cooperating with God's special grace that enlightened you and, through you, the whole world, to the omnipotent and ever-merciful God. You have led souls to trust in the merciful heart of Jesus. You were instrumental in helping us to understand the meaning of the blood and water that flowed from the side of Jesus on the Cross.

The image of Jesus, King of mercy, with His hand raised in blessing, and red and white rays of light streaming from the heart of Jesus, which you saw upon earth and then asked to have painted, is now an instrument to draw souls to Jesus. Millions now appreciate the mercy of Jesus, first bestowed on each one of us in the Sacrament of Baptism, and renewed in the Sacrament of Reconciliation whenever one makes a good confession. Souls are now drawn to the throne of Divine Grace and Mercy, where the Real Presence of Jesus Christ resides in the Eucharist in our tabernacles, and to the altars of the Catholic Church, where the Sacrifice of the Cross is perpetuated.

The hand of Jesus raised in blessing in the Divine Mercy image also reminds me of His merciful forgiveness of sins, as the priest raises his hand in the same way as Jesus in the image, when the priest grants me absolution of sins when I go to confession.

St. Faustina, from heaven you continue to be God's instrument in drawing souls through your

Jesus, I Trust in You

DIVINE MERCY

intercession to the infinite mercy of the Lord. Help me never to doubt God's mercy when I have sinned, but always to say: "Jesus, I trust in You." Amen.

St. Pio of Pietrelcina (Padre Pio)

St. Pio, you lived on earth for fifty years as a living crucifix, with the stigmata of Jesus Christ. The five wounds of Jesus Christ were embedded in your body, and through them you suffered for the conversion of sinners and the glory of God. When you offered the holy Sacrifice of the Mass, the perfume of sanctity filled the church. At your Mass, people were reminded that the celebration of the Holy Eucharist perpetuates the same sacrifice that Jesus Christ offered on the Cross of Calvary two thousand years ago.

You were so dedicated to the Sacrament of Reconciliation and spent hours each day hearing confessions, granting absolution from sin in the name of Jesus Christ. When God willed it, you could read souls and know whether people coming to you for confession were truly sorry for their sins. You then knew if a penitent had a firm purpose of amendment to correct sinful ways.

Intercede for me and for all sinners of the world, St. Pio, that we may come in sorrow to the Sacrament of Reconciliation and appreciate in loving faith that holy Mass offers in, with, and through Jesus Christ the selfsame sacrifice of infinite value, once offered on the Cross of Calvary. Amen.

Prayers of Thanksgiving and Petition

Grace Before Meals

Bless us, O Lord, and these Your gifts, which we are about to receive, from Your bounty through Christ our Lord. Amen.

Grace After Meals

We give You thanks, almighty God, for all Your benefits, You who live and reign, world without end. Amen.

Prayer of an Altar Server

It is a privilege to serve at Your altar, dear God. I believe that during the holy Sacrifice of the Mass the death of Your Son, Jesus Christ, is offered to God the Father. I believe that bread and wine are changed into the living Body, Blood, Soul, and Divinity of my Savior, Jesus Christ.

How happy I am to serve at Your altar, O Lord. I want to prove pleasing to You when I serve, O Jesus. May I never forget that the great happening of holy Mass is the greatest action on earth. Thank You for calling me to serve at Your altar, my Jesus. Amen.

Prayer for Priests and Vocations

Jesus, Lord of the harvest, send laborers to gather Your great harvest. Give us shepherds, for the service of salvation, who do only your work without compromise.

Rekindle in priests the gift of God that was received at ordination. Grant that priests live only in the truth and manner of Jesus Christ. Open their hearts, Lord Jesus, to guard the true faith entrusted to the Church in the Holy Spirit. Keep their hearts prayerful and open to holy purity so as to live always in the love of God the Father, for the salvation of all.

Lord Jesus Christ, our God and Savior, call many to be pastors, to preach the word of God and give us the Bread of Life, the Holy Eucharist, your very Body, Blood, Soul and Divinity, as they perpetuate your Sacrifice.

Mary, Mother of Priests, Mother of holy vocations, you once said "yes" to give us Jesus Christ, the High Priest. Say "yes" to many priestly vocations today.

Mary, Mother of Mercy, mediatrix of grace, intercede that blood and water which gushed from your Son's merciful heart may flow abundantly today upon

MOTHER OF PRIESTS, MOTHER OF VOCATIONS

souls through the priestly administrations of your sons. Obtain for the Church holy priests to wash away sins and bestow to souls a sharing in the life of God through the Holy Eucharist. Amen.

(Composed by Father Robert J. Fox, in gratitude to Jesus and Mary for his fortieth anniversary of ordination, April 24, 1995.)

Prayer of a Sick or Crippled Child for the Conversion of America

Dear Jesus, I believe in faith that You have permitted me to have this weakness of body because You love me. Your heavenly Father sent many sufferings upon You, dear Jesus, out of love for You and for all persons. You accepted Your very great sufferings in reparation for the sins of the whole world. You had no sins Yourself, dear Lord. Yet You suffered more than all mankind. You felt the pain and the loneliness so greatly because You were so great in Your Person, being God Himself.

You have shown Yourself to people in our own times with a heart surrounded with thorns. Your Blessed Mother has shown her Immaculate Heart, also pierced with thorns. Both You, Jesus, and you, Mary, have asked that sacrifices be offered for the conversion of sinners. I thank You, O Jesus, for giving me a very special cross. By uniting my sufferings to those of Jesus and Mary, I can help save souls.

I want to offer my sufferings and prayers for all young people so that they will be holy, pure, and close to You. I offer my sufferings for the conversion of my country. Amen.

Prayer of Healthy Children for Sick Children

Dear Lord God of health and all good things, I thank You for the healthy body You gave me. But I know that You love in a special way those who suffer most. I ask You to give strength to children who are sick, crippled, and lack the power to run and play. Some children also have been born weak in mind. They cannot learn easily. You love them, too, Lord. Every child living on the earth has an immortal soul made in Your own image and likeness. Protect them with Your love and mercy.

I will try to use the powers of my body, dear Lord, for Your honor and glory. Help me also to show Your love to other boys and girls. I must remember that You love them in a special way, and what I do to and for them, dear Jesus, I do to You. Amen.

Act of Sacrifice

O most holy hearts of Jesus and Mary, I beg your mercy. I offer everything I am and do as acts of reparation for sins by which God is offended. I ask for the conversion of sinners. Save them from the fires of hell. I wish to help bring true peace upon my country and the world through the holy hearts of Jesus and Mary. I accept whatever sufferings the Lord will send me. Amen.

Prayer of Self-Denial

Jesus, I want to deny myself. I want to give up this desire I have. I know it would not be a sin to enjoy good things. But I freely give up this pleasure to show my love to You and to satisfy for sins that offend You. I beg the conversion of sinners. Amen.

An Offering of Sufferings

My God, my God, I offer all my sufferings for Your love. I offer all pains of body and mind for Your love, in reparation for the sins committed against the Immaculate Heart of Mary, for the Pope, and for the conversion of sinners. Amen.

Offering of Self to God

O Jesus, I wish to offer myself to God. I promise to accept all the sufferings You may send me. I do this as an act of reparation for the sins by which You are offended. I ask for the conversion of sinners. Amen.

Thanksgiving to God for Graces

My God, I love You. Thank You for the graces You have given me. May I never refuse any grace You offer me. Amen.

Prayer Before a Test

O Mary, Seat of wisdom, help me to use my mind to the best of my ability in taking this test.

Make my mind clear so that I may remember and think correctly.

Jesus, You who are all Truth, help me to know truth, and in the future help me to study so that I may make good use of the mind God has given me. Help me to do my very best in this test. Amen.

Prayer Before Traveling

My God, protect me and all who travel with me from harm. May I see Your beauty in the world as I travel. Keep us safe in body and soul.

Archangel Raphael, you who guided and protected Tobias on his journey, watch over us and see to our every need. Guardian angel of mine, and guardian angels of all who travel with me, pray for us and bring us safely home again. Amen.

Prayer Before a Game

Dear God, help me to do my best in this game of sports. May I think clearly and react quickly and kindly. Help me, dear God, to be a good sport. Help me to show goodness to all others in this game. Help me also to look fairly upon others struggling to win, too.

Dear God, may the victory that will be mine be that which will be for the good of my soul and the souls of others. May I humbly accept the results of this game after doing my best. Keep me from injury and help me to grow strong in body and soul. Amen.

FÁTIMA PRAYERS AND DEVOTIONS

A Pledge to Our Lady of Fátima

Dear Queen and Mother, I want to do everything that you asked us to do when you appeared to the three children at Fátima in 1917. You promised to:

- Convert Russia.
- Bring peace to the world.
- Save souls from hell.

In reparation to your Immaculate Heart for my sins and the sins of the world, I promise to:

- Say the Rosary daily, with my family when possible.
- Wear the Scapular, which makes me a special child of Mary.
- Do my daily duties properly, offering up all the sacrifices necessary to keep from offending God.
- Try to make the five First Saturdays. *(See* The Great Promise for First Saturdays, *below.)*

(The above pledge, which does not bind under pain of sin, will please the Sacred Heart of Jesus and the Immaculate Heart of Mary.)

The Great Promise for First Saturdays

The Catholic Church has approved of Fátima. It is believed that our Blessed Mother appeared in

Fátima, Portugal, in 1917. People were asked by Our Lady to stop sinning. We are asked to do these things on first Saturdays:

- Go to confession and offer the confession in *reparation* for sins committed against the Sacred Heart of Jesus and the Immaculate Heart of Mary.
- Receive Our Lord in Holy Communion, also in *reparation*.
- Pray the holy Rosary — at least five decades, also in *reparation*.
- Meditate on the mysteries of the Rosary for fifteen minutes in *reparation*.

Many Catholics do the above four things, not just for five Saturdays, as Our Lady asked, but every first Saturday. Sister Lucia of Fátima said that Mary spoke to her as follows:

"Look, my daughter, my heart is all pierced with thorns, which men drive into it every moment by their blasphemies and ingratitude.

"Do you at least seek to console me, and let men know that:

"I promise to assist at the hour of death, with the graces necessary for salvation, all those who on the first Saturday of five consecutive months will go to confession, receive Holy Communion, recite the beads, and keep me company during a quarter of an hour, meditating on the . . . mysteries of the Rosary, with the purpose of making reparation."

Prayer to Our Lady of Fátima

O Lady of Fátima, you who did show yourself at Fátima, Portugal, as Our Lady of the Rosary, grant peace to the world. At Fátima, you asked that everyone pray the Rosary properly every day. You asked for sacrifices for sinners so that their souls would not go to hell. At Fátima, you made known that God wants devotion spread in the whole world to your Immaculate Heart.

O Lady of Fátima, you who came from heaven to earth and spoke to three little children, what you told them was for me, too, and for the whole world. You showed your special love for children at Fátima. I will try hard to remember to pray the Rosary daily, to make sacrifices for souls, to pray for the conversion of Russia, for world peace, and for our Holy Father, the Pope, as you asked us. O Lady of Fátima, I love your Immaculate Heart. Amen.

Prayer to God in the Holy Eucharist
(As taught to the Fátima children)

Most Holy Trinity, I adore You! My God, my God, I love You in the Most Blessed Sacrament.

Offering of the Eucharist to the Blessed Trinity
(As taught to the Fátima children)

O most Holy Trinity — Father, Son, and Holy Spirit — I adore You profoundly, I offer You the most precious Body, Blood, Soul, and Divinity of Jesus, present in all the tabernacles of the world, in reparation for the outrages, sacrileges, and indifference by which He is offended. By the infinite merits of the Sacred Heart of Jesus, and the Immaculate Heart of Mary, I beg the conversion of poor sinners. Amen.

Prayer for Pardon
(As taught to the Fátima children)

My God, I believe, I adore, I trust, and I love You! I beg pardon for those who do not believe, do not adore, do not trust, and do not love You *(three times)*.

Wearing of the Brown Scapular of Our Lady

At Fátima, our Blessed Mother encouraged each of us to consecrate ourselves to her Immaculate Heart. The sign of our consecration can be the wearing of the Brown Scapular of Mt. Carmel. The Popes have approved of this also. You should be invested in the Brown Scapular by one with authority to do so. Then you will belong to the Confraternity of the Carmelites while still living in this world. By wearing the Brown Scapular of Our Lady, you may then believe that our heavenly Mother will pray that you are in the state of sanctifying grace, sharing in God's own life, at the moment of your death.

Good mothers give clothing to their children to wear. You are a special child of Mary. By wearing the Brown Scapular of Our Lady of Mt. Carmel, you wear Mary's special clothing that she has given to you. You must then live a good Christian life. Wear your Brown Scapular always, even at night. Mary's prayers will then always protect you, and she will keep you in the love of the Sacred Heart of Jesus.

In addition to the promise of heaven for wearing the Brown Scapular while living a good Catholic life, Mary has promised something more. If we do a little more, we can believe that Mary will also come to deliver us from the fires of purgatory on the first Saturday soon after our death. The little more includes these three things: (1) wearing the Brown Scapular; (2) observing chastity (purity) according to your state in life; and (3) saying a part of the Rosary daily (at least five decades).

Of the Brown Scapular Pope Pius XII said, "Let it be your sign of consecration to the Immaculate Heart of Mary, which we are particularly urging in these dangerous times."

Pope Paul VI said after Vatican II, "Ever hold in great esteem the practices and exercises of the devotion to the most Blessed Virgin which have been recommended for centuries by the Magisterium of the Church. And among them we judge well to recall especially the Marian Rosary and the religious use of the Scapular of Mt. Carmel."

Pope Paul VI also said, "It is permitted to preach . . . that the Blessed Virgin will aid the souls of the brothers and sisters of the Confraternity of the Blessed Virgin of Mt. Carmel after their death by her continual intercession, by her suffrages and merits, and by her special protection, especially on . . . Saturday, which is the day especially dedicated by the Church to the same Blessed Virgin Mary."

One who dies wearing the Brown Scapular of Our Lady and has said the Rosary during life, praying repeatedly, "pray for us sinners now and at the hour of our death," can believe that the Mother of God will intervene at the moment of death for the salvation of one's soul.

ASPIRATIONS

(Aspirations are short prayers we can whisper to God during the day as we do our work or have recreation. Think of God often during the day in short prayers. The following are sample prayers. In time you may memorize your favorites. If you join any of the following aspirations or a similar invocation to some good action, raising your heart and mind to God in humble hope, Mother Church will also grant you a partial indulgence. To gain the indulgence of the Church, you can make any such pious prayer to raise the intention of your ordinary actions to God.)

- May Jesus Christ be praised.
- Lord, I believe in You.
- Lord, I adore You.
- Lord, I place my trust in You.
- I love You, my God.
- All for You, most Sacred Heart of Jesus.
- Your will be done.
- As the Lord wills.
- God, help me.
- Comfort me, my Jesus.
- Graciously hear my prayer, O Lord.
- My Jesus, save me.
- My Jesus, have mercy on me.
- Mercy, my Jesus.
- Jesus, do not permit me to be separated from You.
- Do not abandon me, my Jesus.
- Hail Mary, full of grace.
- Glory to God in the highest.
- Great are You, O Lord.
- Praise the Lord.
- May the Holy Trinity be blessed.
- Heart of Jesus, burning with love for us, inflame our hearts with love for You.
- Sacred Heart of Jesus, all for You.
- Most Sacred Heart of Jesus, have mercy on us.
- My God and my all.
- God, have mercy on me, a sinner.
- Teach me to do Your will, because You are my God.

- Lord, may we be of one mind in truth and of one heart in charity.
- Lord, increase our faith.
- Lord, save us; we are perishing.
- My Lord and my God. *(This should be said silently at the elevation of the sacred host and the chalice during Mass.)*
- Sweet heart of Mary, be my salvation.
- Glory be to the Father, and to the Son, and to the Holy Spirit.
- Jesus, Mary, Joseph, assist me in my last agony.
- Jesus, Mary, Joseph, may I sleep and rest in peace with you.
- Jesus, meek and humble of heart, make my heart like Your heart.
- May the Most Blessed Sacrament be praised and adored forever.
- Stay with us, O Lord.
- Mother of sorrows, pray for us.
- Sorrowful and Immaculate Heart of Mary, I consecrate myself to you.
- Immaculate Heart of Mary, I love you.
- My Mother, my hope.
- Jesus, Mary, Joseph, I love you; save souls.
- Our Lady of Mt. Carmel, pray for us. Our Lady of the Brown Scapular, protect us.
- Our Lady of Lourdes, pray for us.
- Our Lady of Fátima, obtain peace for the world.
- Savior of the world, save Russia.
- St. Michael the Archangel, defend us in battle.

- My guardian angel, be with me always.
- Most Blessed Trinity, I adore You.
- My God, my God, I love You in the Most Blessed Sacrament.
- My dear Lord Jesus, I love You. I want to love You more each day.
- O Sacrament most holy, O Sacrament divine, all praise and all thanksgiving be every moment Thine.
- My Mother, keep me from mortal sin this day (night).
- All for You, most Sacred Heart of Jesus.
- Come to me, O Jesus, as I come to You.
- Jesus, be my salvation.
- My Jesus, I ask for the grace never to commit mortal sin.
- Holy hearts of Jesus and Mary, this is for love of you.
- Holy hearts of Jesus and Mary, I offer this in reparation to you.
- My Jesus, this is for love of You, for the conversion of sinners, and in reparation for sins committed against the Immaculate Heart of Mary *(when making a sacrifice)*.
- My Jesus, forgive us our sins, lead all souls to heaven, especially those most in need of Your mercy.
- My Jesus, I offer this Holy Communion in reparation for the conversion of sinners.
- My Jesus, my Mother, I offer this confession in reparation for my sins and those of the whole world.

- My Jesus, I adore profoundly Your Real Presence in the Most Blessed Sacrament.
- My Jesus, I believe that every holy Mass perpetuates the Sacrifice of the Cross.
- Heavenly Father, I offer You the sacred Body and most precious Blood of Your Son, Jesus Christ.
- Almighty God, give me graces through the Immaculate Heart of Mary.
- May the hearts of Jesus and Mary be venerated everywhere.
- Jesus, it is for love of You, for the conversion of sinners, for the Holy Father, and in reparation for the sins committed against the Immaculate Heart of Mary *(when making a sacrifice)*.

LITANIES

Litany of the Most Sacred Heart of Jesus

Lord, have mercy.
Christ, have mercy.
Lord, have mercy.
Christ, hear us.
Christ, graciously hear us.

God the Father of heaven, have mercy on us.
God the Son, Redeemer of the world, have mercy on us.
God the Holy Spirit, have mercy on us.
Holy Trinity, one God, have mercy on us.

Heart of Jesus, Son of the eternal Father, have mercy on us.

Heart of Jesus, formed by the Holy Spirit in the womb of the Virgin Mother, have mercy on us.

Heart of Jesus, substantially united to the Word of God, have mercy on us.

Heart of Jesus, of infinite majesty, have mercy on us.

Heart of Jesus, sacred temple of God, have mercy on us.

Heart of Jesus, tabernacle of the Most High, have mercy on us.

Heart of Jesus, house of God and gate of heaven, have mercy on us.

Heart of Jesus, burning furnace of charity, have mercy on us.

Heart of Jesus, abode of justice and love, have mercy on us.

Heart of Jesus, full of goodness and love, have mercy on us.

Heart of Jesus, abyss of all virtues, have mercy on us.

Heart of Jesus, most worthy of all praise, have mercy on us.

Heart of Jesus, king and center of all praise, have mercy on us.

Heart of Jesus, king and center of all hearts, have mercy on us.

Heart of Jesus, in whom are all the treasures of wisdom and knowledge, have mercy on us.

Heart of Jesus, in whom dwells the fullness of divinity, have mercy on us.

Heart of Jesus, in whom the Father is well pleased, have mercy on us.

Heart of Jesus, of whose fullness we have all received, have mercy on us.

Heart of Jesus, desire of the everlasting hills, have mercy on us.

Heart of Jesus, patient and most merciful, have mercy on us.

Heart of Jesus, enriching all who invoke You, have mercy on us.

Heart of Jesus, fountain of life and holiness, have mercy on us.

Heart of Jesus, propitiation for our sins, have mercy on us.

Heart of Jesus, loaded down with opprobrium, have mercy on us.

Heart of Jesus, bruised for our offenses, have mercy on us.

Heart of Jesus, obedient unto death, have mercy on us.

Heart of Jesus, pierced with a lance, have mercy on us.

Heart of Jesus, source of all consolation, have mercy on us.

Heart of Jesus, our life and resurrection, have mercy on us.

Heart of Jesus, our peace and reconciliation, have mercy on us.

Heart of Jesus, victim for our sins, have mercy on us.

Heart of Jesus, salvation of those who trust in You, have mercy on us.

Heart of Jesus, hope of those who die in You, have mercy on us.

Heart of Jesus, delight of all the saints, have mercy on us.

V. Lamb of God, who takes away the sins of the world.

R. Spare us, O Lord.

V. Lamb of God, who takes away the sins of the world.

R. Graciously hear us, O Lord.

V. Lamb of God, who takes away the sins of the world.

R. Have mercy on us.

V. Jesus, meek and humble of heart.

R. Make our hearts like Yours.

Let us pray: Almighty and eternal God, look upon the heart of Your most beloved Son and upon the praises and satisfaction which He offers You in the name of sinners; and to those who implore Your mercy, in Your great goodness, grant them forgiveness in the Name of the same Jesus Christ, Your Son, who lives and reigns with You forever and ever.

R. Amen.

Litany of the Holy Spirit

Lord, have mercy on us.
Christ, have mercy on us.
Lord, have mercy on us.

God our Father, Creator, have mercy on us.
God the Son, our Redeemer, have mercy on us.
God the Holy Spirit, Sanctifier, have mercy on us.

> **V.** God the Father, send us the Holy Spirit.
> **R.** We pray You, Lord.
> **V.** God the Son, give us the Holy Spirit.
> **R.** We pray You, Lord.
> **V.** God the Holy Spirit, fill the hearts of your faithful.
> **R.** We pray You, Lord.

Holy Spirit, who proceeds from the Father and the Son, have mercy on us.
Holy Spirit, the Lord and Giver of life, have mercy on us.
Holy Spirit, worshiped and glorified with the Father and the Son, have mercy on us.
Holy Spirit, Co-Creator of heaven and earth, have mercy on us.
Holy Spirit, who overshadowed the Blessed Virgin Mary and gave us Jesus Christ our Lord, have mercy on us.
Holy Spirit, Source of wisdom and understanding, have mercy on us.

Holy Spirit, Source of counsel and fortitude, have mercy on us.

Holy Spirit, Source of knowledge and holiness, have mercy on us.

Holy Spirit, Soul of the Holy Roman Catholic Church, have mercy on us.

Holy Spirit, Guide and Protector of the one, holy, catholic, and apostolic Church, have mercy on us.

Holy Spirit, Gift of the Father to Peter and the Apostles and their lawful successors, have mercy on us.

Holy Spirit, Gift of the Father to priests, deacons, and religious who have vowed their lives to God, have mercy on us.

Holy Spirit, Gift of true faith, hope, and charity to all who accept You, have mercy on us.

Holy Spirit, Giver of true charismatic gifts, have mercy on us.

Holy Spirit, Giver of perseverance in true faith and knowledge, have mercy on us.

Holy Spirit, Giver of the gift of consolation, have mercy on us.

Holy Spirit, who instructs the hearts of the faithful, have mercy on us.

Holy Spirit, who helps us relish what is right and what is just, have mercy on us.

Holy Spirit, who helps us call God "Abba," our Father, have mercy on us.

Holy Spirit, who helps us accept Jesus as our
Brother and Savior, have mercy on us.
Holy Spirit, who helps us accept Your guidance
and dwells in the hearts of the faithful, have
mercy on us.
Holy Spirit, Regenerator and Renovator of the
hearts of the faithful, have mercy on us.
Holy Spirit, dwelling in our souls by sanctifying
grace, have mercy on us.

Holy Spirit, graciously hear us.
Holy Spirit, respond to our cry.
Holy Spirit, renew the face of the earth.

Let us pray: Come, Holy Spirit, fill the hearts of
Your faithful, and kindle in us the fire of Your love.
R. Amen.

Litany of the Blessed Virgin Mary
(Also called the Litany of Loreto)

Lord, have mercy.
Christ, have mercy.
Lord, have mercy.
Christ, hear us.
Christ, graciously hear us.

God the Father of heaven, have mercy on us.
God the Son, Redeemer of the world, have mercy
on us.

God the Holy Spirit, have mercy on us.
Holy Trinity, one God, have mercy on us.

Holy Mary, pray for us.
Holy Mother of God, pray for us.
Holy Virgin of virgins, pray for us.
Mother of Christ, pray for us.
Mother of divine grace, pray for us.
Mother most pure, pray for us.
Mother most chaste, pray for us.
Mother inviolate, pray for us.
Mother undefiled, pray for us.
Mother most amiable, pray for us.
Mother most admirable, pray for us.
Mother of good counsel, pray for us.
Mother of our Creator, pray for us.
Mother of our Savior, pray for us.
Virgin most prudent, pray for us.
Virgin most venerable, pray for us.
Virgin most renowned, pray for us.
Virgin most powerful, pray for us.
Virgin most merciful, pray for us.
Virgin most faithful, pray for us.
Mirror of justice, pray for us.
Seat of wisdom, pray for us.
Cause of our joy, pray for us.
Spiritual vessel, pray for us.
Vessel of honor, pray for us.
Singular vessel of devotion, pray for us.
Mystical rose, pray for us.

Tower of David, pray for us.
Tower of ivory, pray for us.
House of gold, pray for us.
Ark of the covenant, pray for us.
Gate of heaven, pray for us.
Morning star, pray for us.
Health of the sick, pray for us.
Refuge of sinners, pray for us.
Comforter of the afflicted, pray for us.
Help of Christians, pray for us.
Queen of angels, pray for us.
Queen of patriarchs, pray for us.
Queen of prophets, pray for us.
Queen of Apostles, pray for us.
Queen of martyrs, pray for us.
Queen of confessors, pray for us.
Queen of virgins, pray for us.
Queen of all saints, pray for us.
Queen conceived without original sin, pray for us.
Queen assumed into heaven, pray for us.
Queen of the most holy Rosary, pray for us.
Queen of families, pray for us.
Queen of peace, pray for us.

> **V.** Lamb of God, who takes away the sins of
> the world.
> **R.** Spare us, O Lord.
> **V.** Lamb of God, who takes away the sins of
> the world.
> **R.** Graciously hear us, O Lord.

V. Lamb of God, who takes away the sins of
the world.
R. Have mercy on us.

V. Pray for us, O holy Mother of God.
R. That we may be made worthy of the
promises of Christ.

Let us pray: Grant, we beg You, O Lord God,
that we Your servants may enjoy lasting health of
mind and body, and by the glorious intercession of
the Blessed Mary, ever Virgin, be delivered from present sorrow and enter into the joy of eternal happiness. Through Christ our Lord.
R. Amen.

Litany of the Immaculate Heart of Mary

Lord, have mercy.
Christ, have mercy.
Lord, have mercy.
Christ, hear us.
Christ, graciously hear us.

God the Father of heaven, have mercy on us.
God the Son, Redeemer of the world, have mercy
on us.
God the Holy Spirit, have mercy on us.
Holy Trinity, one God, have mercy on us.

Immaculate Heart of Mary, most like the Sacred
   Heart of Jesus, pray for us.

Immaculate Heart of Mary, whose soul was created
   without original sin, pray for us.

Immaculate Heart of Mary, who said to God's
   messenger, "Be it done to me according to your
   word," pray for us.

Immaculate Heart of Mary, who always remained
   sinless, pray for us.

Immaculate Heart of Mary, to whom the angel
   Gabriel first announced the Good News, pray
   for us.

Immaculate Heart of Mary, who awaited the Savior
   with the greatest love, pray for us.

Immaculate Heart of Mary, within whom we see
   the beginning of the Church, pray for us.

Immaculate Heart of Mary, who remained always a
   Virgin in giving us Jesus, pray for us.

Immaculate Heart of Mary, Queen of peace, who
   gave us the Prince of peace, pray for us.

Immaculate Heart of Mary, who conceived Jesus in
   your heart before conceiving Him in your
   womb, pray for us.

Immaculate Heart of Mary, who first adored the
   newborn Savior, pray for us.

Immaculate Heart of Mary, Mother of love in the
   Holy Family at Nazareth, pray for us.

Immaculate Heart of Mary, whose immaculate soul
   and virginal body were taken into heaven, pray
   for us.

Immaculate Heart of Mary, Mother of God and Mother of us all, pray for us.

Immaculate Heart of Mary, Queen of guardian angels, pray for us.

Immaculate Heart of Mary, Queen of all angels and saints, pray for us.

Immaculate Heart of Mary, who kept the Word of God in your heart, pray for us.

Immaculate Heart of Mary, whose soul Simeon said a sword would pierce, pray for us.

Immaculate Heart of Mary, praying with the Apostles for the Church, pray for us.

Immaculate Heart of Mary, desiring sacrifices for the conversion of sinners, pray for us.

Immaculate Heart of Mary, comfort to souls at the hour of death, pray for us.

Immaculate Heart of Mary, at whose request Jesus changed water into wine, pray for us.

Immaculate Heart of Mary, offering Jesus in sacrifice on Mt. Calvary, pray for us.

Immaculate Heart of Mary, and Our Lady of the Most Holy Eucharist, pray for us.

Immaculate Heart of Mary, teacher of us in the way of God, pray for us.

Immaculate Heart of Mary, living example of the love of humility, pray for us.

Immaculate Heart of Mary, perfect model of adoring the Father through Christ in the Spirit, pray for us.

Immaculate Heart of Mary, Mother of the Church
and spouse of the Holy Spirit, pray for us.

Immaculate Heart of Mary, Mother of Christ and
our Mother in the Communion of Saints, pray
for us.

Immaculate Heart of Mary, crowned as Queen in
heaven by the Most Blessed Trinity, pray for us.

Immaculate Heart of Mary, praying for our
salvation, pray for us.

Immaculate Heart of Mary, full of grace and
Mother of grace, pray for us.

Immaculate Heart of Mary, desiring to give grace
to children who ask, pray for us.

Immaculate Heart of Mary, ever ready to hear the
prayers of children, pray for us.

Immaculate Heart of Mary, wounded in love by
the sins of men, pray for us.

Immaculate Heart of Mary, hope and comfort for
merciful forgiveness, pray for us.

Immaculate Heart of Mary, perfect model of
reparation, pray for us.

Immaculate Heart of Mary, triumph of all who
believe in God's word, pray for us.

V. Pray for us, O holy Mother of God.
R. That we may be made worthy of the
promises of Christ.

Let us pray: O sorrowful and Immaculate Heart
of Mary, Mother and model of the Church, I want

to bring comfort to your all-pure heart wounded by sin. I offer this litany, my sufferings, and good works of this day in reparation for the sins of the world. Through Jesus Christ, you are the cause of our joy and the means of salvation. I shall try to spread devotion to your Immaculate Heart so that many souls will find salvation in the Sacred Heart of your Son.

R. Amen.

Litany of St. Joseph

Lord, have mercy.
Christ, have mercy.
Lord, have mercy.
Christ, hear us.
Christ, graciously hear us.

God the Father of heaven, have mercy on us.
God the Son, Redeemer of the world, have mercy on us.
God the Holy Spirit, have mercy on us.
Holy Trinity, one God, have mercy on us.

Holy Mary, pray for us.
St. Joseph, pray for us.
Renowned offspring of David, pray for us.
Light of patriarchs, pray for us.
Spouse of the Mother of God, pray for us.
Chaste guardian of the Virgin, pray for us.
Foster father of the Son of God, pray for us.

Diligent protector of Christ, pray for us.
Head of the Holy Family, pray for us.
Joseph most just, pray for us.
Joseph most chaste, pray for us.
Joseph most prudent, pray for us.
Joseph most strong, pray for us.
Joseph most obedient, pray for us.
Joseph most faithful, pray for us.
Mirror of patience, pray for us.
Lover of poverty, pray for us.
Model of artisans, pray for us.
Glory of home life, pray for us.

St. Joseph and the Christ Child

Guardian of virgins, pray for us.
Pillar of families, pray for us.
Solace of the wretched, pray for us.
Hope of the sick, pray for us.
Patron of the dying, pray for us.
Terror of demons, pray for us.
Protector of Holy Church, pray for us.

> **V.** Lamb of God, who takes away the sins of the world.
> **R.** Spare us, O Lord.
> **V.** Lamb of God, who takes away the sins of the world.
> **R.** Graciously hear us, O Lord.
> **V.** Lamb of God, who takes away the sins of the world.
> **R.** Have mercy on us.

> **V.** He made him the lord of his household.
> **R.** And prince over all his possessions.

Let us pray: O God, in Your ineffable providence You were pleased to choose Blessed Joseph to be the spouse of Your most holy Mother. Grant, we beg You, that we may be worthy to have him for our intercessor in heaven, whom on earth we venerate as our protector. You who live and reign forever and ever.

> **R.** Amen.

Litany of My Guardian Angel

Lord, have mercy on us.

Christ, have mercy on us.

Lord, have mercy on us.

Christ, hear us.

Christ, graciously hear us.

God the Father of heaven, have mercy on us.

God the Son, Redeemer of the world, have mercy
on us.

God the Holy Spirit, have mercy on us.

Holy Trinity, one God, have mercy on us.

Holy Mary, pray for us.

Queen of heaven, pray for us.

Angel, my guardian, pray for me.

Holy Angel, my protector in all dangers, pray for
me.

Holy Angel, my defense in all afflictions, pray for
me.

Holy Angel, most faithful lover, pray for me.

Holy Angel, my preceptor, pray for me.

Holy Angel, my guide, pray for me.

Holy Angel, witness of all my actions, pray for me.

Holy Angel, my helper in all my difficulties, pray
for me.

Holy Angel, my negotiator with God, pray for me.

Holy Angel, my advocate, pray for me.

Holy Angel, lover of chastity, pray for me.

Holy Angel, lover of innocence, pray for me.

Holy Angel, most obedient to God, pray for me.

Holy Angel, director of my soul, pray for me.

Holy Angel, model of purity, pray for me.

Holy Angel, model of docility, pray for me.

Holy Angel, my counselor in doubt, pray for me.

Holy Angel, my guardian through life, pray for me.

Holy Angel, my shield at the hour of death, pray for me.

V. Lamb of God, who takes away the sins of the world.

R. Spare us, O Lord.

V. Lamb of God, who takes away the sins of the world.

R. Graciously hear us, O Lord.

V. Lamb of God, who takes away the sins of the world.

R. Have mercy on us.

V. Be the Savior of Your faithful people, Lord.

R. Grant them your blessing, for they belong to You.

ACTS OF CONSECRATION AND REPARATION

Act of Consecration to the Sacred Heart of Jesus

Sacred Heart of Jesus, take me, for I am Yours. I wish to make reparation for all the sins of the world, including my own. I wish to offer the same satisfaction that You once made to Your eternal Father on the Cross. You continue to renew this same offering daily on our Catholic altars. I offer this in union with the Immaculate Heart of Your Mother.

O loving Jesus, through the intercession of the Blessed Virgin Mother, our model in reparation, receive the offering and consecration I now make of myself to You. Keep me faithful unto death. Bring me one day to that happy home in heaven. I desire to live forever with God the Father and the Holy Spirit and You, my Jesus. Amen.

Act of Consecration to the Immaculate Heart of Mary

Immaculate Heart of Mary, I consecrate my entire self to your love. All that I am and all that I have belong to you, dear Mother Mary. I consecrate to you my heart, my eyes, my hands, my feet. I give you my thoughts, my mind, my will, all my property and possessions.

I ask your dear loving heart, my Mother, for special graces that God gives through you from the Sacred Heart of Jesus. I ask for graces not only for myself but also for the whole world. Together, with you, O Immaculate Heart, I offer to my heavenly Father the sacred Body and precious Blood of Jesus present in all the tabernacles of the world.

I am all Yours, and all that I have is Yours, O most loving Jesus, through the Immaculate Heart of Mary, Your Mother. Amen.

Act of Total Consecration to Mary

(This total act of consecration, originally made by St. Louis de Montfort, should be made only after a time of serious study and careful preparation. One should first get advice from some person known for deep devotion to Mary. The spirit of the consecration should thereafter be lived in one's daily life.)

I, _____, a faithless sinner, renew and ratify today in your hands, O Immaculate Mother, the vows of my baptism; I renounce forever Satan, his pomps and works; and I give myself entirely to Jesus Christ, the Incarnate Wisdom, to carry my cross after Him all the days of my life, and to be more faithful to Him than I have ever been before.

In the presence of all the heavenly court, I choose you this day for my Mother and Mistress. I deliver and consecrate to you, as your slave, my body and soul, my goods, both interior and exterior, and even the value of all my good actions, past, present and future; leaving to you the entire and full right of disposing of me, and all that belongs to me, without exception, according to your good pleasure, for the greater glory of God, in time and in eternity. Amen.

Act of Consecration to the Holy Guardian Angel

Holy Guardian Angel, you continually behold the face of our Father in heaven! God entrusted me to you from the beginning of my life. I thank you with all my heart for your loving care. I commit myself to you and promise you my love and fidelity.

I beg you: Protect me against my own weakness and against the attacks of the wicked spirits; enlighten my mind and heart so that I may always know and accomplish the will of God; and lead me to union with God the Father, the Son, and the Holy Spirit. Amen.

(This form of consecration has been approved by the Vatican.)

Daily Sacrifices in Reparation

It is reported that Our Lady of Fátima showed herself as the sorrowful and Immaculate Heart of Mary. Mary smiled at Fátima only once. She smiled when she said to the children, "God is pleased with your sacrifices." The angel of peace told the children, "Pray! Pray a great deal! The hearts of Jesus and Mary have designs of mercy for you. Offer up prayers and sacrifices to the Most High." When Lucia asked, "How are we to make sacrifices?" the angel answered, "Make everything you do a sacrifice, and offer it as an act of reparation for the sins by which He is offended, and in supplication for the conversion of sinners. . . ." Here are simple ways to make sacrifices.

- **Silence:** Spend some special time each day thinking about God. Do not shout or slam doors. The TV, radio, or computer does not always have to be on. Keep quiet when told to. Offer these things up in reparation.
- **Purity:** Turn your thoughts away from bad things. Guard your eyes, your hands, your talk. Do not read or look at bad things. Keep your mind on beauty. Keep busy. Turn bad conversations to good talk. Offer it all in reparation.
- **Friendliness:** Be a friend to the boy or girl others avoid. Make others happy, especially those who are lonely. Make others happy by inviting them to games. Never refuse to talk to people when you should talk. Be a friend as you would be to Jesus.
- **Cleanliness:** Keep your body clean because it is God's temple. Keep your clothes neat. Don't drag dirt into your home or school by dirty shoes. Keep your room clean. Do these things for love of the hearts of Jesus and Mary.
- **Patience:** Hold your temper when you think others accuse you wrongly. Offer it up to Jesus who suffered so much. Keep trying when things are hard. Offer up sickness and hurts. Bear with the mistakes of others with love.
- **Obedience:** Obey immediately, not when you feel like it. By obeying, make your home and classroom a happy place. When you obey

those in authority, see in them the authority of God whom you obey. In reparation, obey as Jesus obeyed God the Father.

- **Study:** Do not be lazy in study. Apply yourself, doing your best. Do not daydream in school; pay attention. Do not waste time. Do it for love of God.
- **Humility:** Admit when you are wrong. Ask others to forgive you. Do not be jealous at the gifts others have. Accept scoldings. Seek God's will, not your own. Do not show off. When tempted against humility, remain humble in reparation.
- **Thankfulness:** Show appreciation to those who are kind to you. This includes your own parents and family members. Thank Jesus in the Blessed Sacrament for His love and presence. Thank God at Mass for all things.
- **Prayers:** In addition to the above good works in reparation, offer special prayers in reparation. Visit Our Lord in the Most Blessed Sacrament.

To Give Oneself to Jesus

Beloved Jesus,
Grant that I rest in You above all things,
above all creatures,
above all Your angels,
above all praise,
above all rejoicing and exultation,

above all glory and honor,
above all heavenly hosts,
for You alone are the Most High,
You alone are the Almighty and Good above all
    things.
May You come to me and relieve me,
and release me from my chains,
and grant me freedom,
because without You my joy is not complete,
without You my table is empty.

THE ROSARY

How to Pray the Rosary

On page 164 is a picture showing how the Rosary is prayed. (See page 167 for sample meditations of the mysteries of the Rosary.)

Starting with the Apostles' Creed ("I believe in God . . .") on the Crucifix, one proceeds to the first bead, saying the Our Father. Then a Hail Mary is said on the next three beads. After each decade, as well as after the first three Hail Marys (following the Glory Be to the Father), say: "O my Jesus, forgive us our sins, save us from the fire of hell, and lead all souls to heaven, especially those who have most need of Your mercy."

The first mystery is announced at this point; if the Glorious Mysteries, for example, are being meditated on, the following or similar words would be

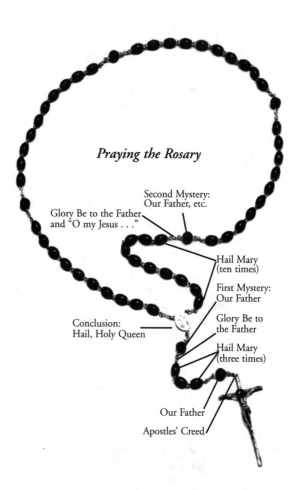

Praying the Rosary

Second Mystery:
Our Father, etc.

Glory Be to the Father
and "O my Jesus . . ."

Hail Mary
(ten times)

First Mystery:
Our Father

Glory Be to
the Father

Conclusion:
Hail, Holy Queen

Hail Mary
(three times)

Our Father

Apostles' Creed

said: "The first Glorious Mystery: The Resurrection."
This is followed by the Our Father, ten Hail Marys,
the Glory Be, "O my Jesus . . . ," and then the second mystery.

The same sequence is followed until all mysteries have been announced, ending the Rosary with
the prayer Hail, Holy Queen. Below are the mysteries of the Rosary:

The Joyful Mysteries
(Mondays and Saturdays)

1. The Annunciation to Mary
2. The Visitation of Mary
3. The Nativity of Our Lord
4. The Presentation of Our Lord
5. The Finding in the Temple

The Luminous Mysteries
(Thursdays)

1. The Baptism of Our Lord
2. The Wedding Feast at Cana
3. The Preaching of the Kingdom of God
4. The Transfiguration of Our Lord
5. The Institution of the Holy Eucharist

The Sorrowful Mysteries
(Tuesdays and Fridays)

1. The Agony in the Garden
2. The Scourging at the Pillar
3. The Crowning With Thorns

4. The Carrying of the Cross
5. The Crucifixion of Our Lord

The Glorious Mysteries
(Sundays and Wednesdays)

1. The Resurrection of Our Lord
2. The Ascension of Our Lord
3. The Descent of the Holy Spirit
4. The Assumption of the Blessed Virgin
5. The Coronation of Mary

A Method of Praying the Rosary
(The Eucharistic Rosary)

- **Holding the Crucifix:** Pray the Apostles' Creed.
- **First Our Father:** This reminds us of one God, and of one true Church.
- **Three Hail Marys:** These remind us of three Persons in God, and also of faith, hope, and charity.

The Rosary is divided into four parts: the Joyful, the Luminous, the Sorrowful, and the Glorious Mysteries. There are five events to each of the four parts. One Our Father and ten Hail Marys are prayed while thinking of each of the events or mysteries. A complete Rosary of all the mysteries would include two hundred Hail Marys. We think of one event or mystery while we pray each set of ten Hail Marys. Our Blessed Mother herself has asked us to pray the Rosary each day while meditating on the mysteries, as have many Popes. Normally, this means at least one set of the mysteries per day. The following are suggested meditations to place your mind and soul in the presence of each mystery while you pray a set of ten Hail Marys after the Our Father.

The Joyful Mysteries
— Mondays and Saturdays

1. The Annunciation to Mary: The angel Gabriel announces to Mary that she is to be the Mother of the Savior. When Mary says, "Be it done unto me according to your word," Jesus comes down from heaven and lives in Mary's womb. At the words of the priest at Mass, Jesus comes down, as the bread and wine are changed into His Body, Blood, Soul, and Divinity. Bread and wine and changed into the same Body and Blood that Mary gave Jesus. In praying these next ten Hail Marys, O Mother Mary, lend me your Immaculate heart to prepare my soul to receive Jesus worthily.

2. The Visitation of Mary: When Mary visits her cousin Elizabeth, she is greeted with, "Why should I be honored with a visit from my Lord?" In welcoming Mary, we also welcome her Son, Jesus. From within the holy womb of Mary, Jesus takes away the original sin of John the Baptist, who is still in the womb of Elizabeth. Mother Mary, come to me, and bring to me your Son, Jesus, as you brought Him to Elizabeth and John. I am anxious to have Jesus visit me in the Mass and receive Him in Holy Communion.

3. The Nativity of Our Lord: Jesus comes into the world from holy Mary like crystal light passing through a clear substance. Mary is the first to adore the newborn Savior, who is Christ our Lord. With St. Joseph, the angels and the shepherds adore Him. My Jesus, I want You to be born into my soul again and again. At every Mass and Holy Communion, You are born anew. I want to prepare to receive You, my Jesus, with a pure heart, the way Mary prepared to receive You.

4. The Presentation of Our Lord: Poor St. Joseph and holy Mary bring the Child Jesus to the Temple at Jerusalem. The prophet Simeon takes the Christ Child into his arms. He says to Mary, "Your own soul a sword shall pierce." As Mary had to suffer for her faith in Jesus, so must we be ready to suffer and make reparation. Simeon could only receive Jesus into his arms, but I can receive Jesus into my soul in Holy Communion.

5. The Finding in the Temple: How full of joy are St. Joseph and holy Mary when they find the twelve-year-old whom they lost. Jesus says that they find Him in the Temple because He has to be "about [His] Father's business." Still today, we find Jesus in church. At the holy Sacrifice of the Mass, Jesus is about His Father's work. At Mass and the Sacraments I grow in faith, love, and grace. I find Jesus this way.

The Luminous Mysteries
(or Mysteries of Light) — Thursdays

1. The Baptism of Our Lord: Christ descends into the waters, the innocent one who becomes "sin" for our sake, as St. Paul says. The heavens open wide and the voice of God the Father declares Jesus to be the beloved Son of God. The Holy Spirit descends to invest Him with the mission that He is to carry out for the salvation of all the world. Lord Jesus, give me light to know and do the mission in my life to which God has called me, so that the Father may be pleased with my life.

2. The Wedding Feast at Cana: At Cana, Jesus raises marriage to the dignity of a sacrament between a Christian man and a Christian woman. Mary says, "Do whatever He tells you." Christ changes water into wine and opens the hearts of the disciples to faith, thanks to the intervention of Mary, the first among believers. If Jesus changes water into wine, then we can believe that He can change bread and wine into His Body and Blood. Lord Jesus, open my heart that I may always have faith in You as Lord, God, and Savior, and influence others to the same faith. May Mary be my model in leading me and others to faith in her divine Incarnate Son.

3. The Preaching of the Kingdom of God: In this mystery we see the preaching by which Jesus proclaims the coming of the Kingdom of God and calls all to conversion. Jesus forgives the sins of all who draw near to Him in humble trust. As Jesus announces that the Kingdom of God is among us, He begins His ministry of mercy. Jesus still shows us mercy today, especially through the Sacrament of Reconciliation (Penance), whereby He gave the Apostles, His first bishops and priests, the power to forgive sins in His name. Mary Magdalene, converted by Jesus from a life of sin, then becomes a great saint and anoints the Body of Jesus with costly perfume to prepare His Body for burial.

4. The Transfiguration of Our Lord: The mystery of light par excellence is the Transfiguration on Mt. Tabor before Peter, James, and John. The glory of Jesus' Godhead shines forth from the face of Christ as the Father commands the astonished Apostles to "listen to Him." They are being prepared to experience with Him the agony of the Passion. They then can come with Him to the joy of the Resurrection and a life transfigured by the Holy Spirit. Lord Jesus, may I so live as one day to share in Your glory in heaven, which was prefigured at Your Transfiguration. I offer this Rosary for all families to come to living faith on earth so as one day to live in Your glory in heaven.

5. The Institution of the Holy Eucharist: A final mystery of light is the institution of the Holy Eucharist. At the Last Supper, Jesus offers His Body and Blood as food under the signs of bread and wine. Thus, Jesus testifies "to the end" His love for humanity, for whose salvation He will offer Himself in sacrifice on the Cross. Lord Jesus, may I always believe that You perpetuate Your Sacrifice of the Cross at every Holy Mass with its infinite merits. Participating in the holy Sacrifice of the Mass is like standing with the apostle John and our Blessed Mother beneath the Cross on Calvary. May I always remember this when I am at Holy Mass. Jesus, may my faith know Your Real Presence with Your Body, Blood, Soul, and Divinity in the consecrated host and consecrated wine, which are transubstantiated into Your very self when the priest says, "This my Body. . . . This is my Blood."

The Sorrowful Mysteries
— Tuesdays and Fridays

1. **The Agony in the Garden:** Right after the first holy Mass of the Last Supper, Jesus goes out into the garden. He becomes very sorrowful. He is suffering already. He begins to sweat blood for the sins of the world. An angel appears holding a chalice to strengthen Him. This chalice is a symbol of the Sacrifice of the Mass, which makes it possible for me to be present at Jesus' Sacrifice of the Cross. Help me, Immaculate Mother of God, to love the mystery of the Mass.

2. **The Scourging at the Pillar:** Jesus sheds His precious Blood when soldiers beat Him cruelly with whips. Jesus is making reparation for sins of the flesh. In every holy Mass, Jesus makes present His precious Blood in the chalice. At Mass, Jesus offers His Blood to God the Father. By the merits of the precious

Blood of Jesus, I am able to receive the love of Jesus, and to offer it for the conversion of sinners.

3. The Crowning With Thorns: The soldiers make a crown out of big thorns and pound it into the head of Jesus. Jesus is making reparation for the sins of coldness and sacrilege that people heap on Him. At every holy Mass, Jesus, who is our true King, becomes present in the Most Blessed Sacrament. He offers at Mass the Sacrifice He offered long ago on Calvary. The hearts of Jesus and Mary are often wounded by the thorns of sin, just as the head of Jesus was wounded with thick thorns. At every holy Mass, I can offer the crucified Jesus to the Most Holy Trinity.

4. The Carrying of the Cross: Jesus carries the heavy Cross up the hill of Calvary. Jesus receives some comfort when along the way He meets His holy Mother. Then Veronica wipes His bloody face. At holy Mass, I can be like another Mary and Veronica and bring comfort to Jesus as He offers the Sacrifice of the Cross through the Holy Eucharist.

5. The Crucifixion of Our Lord: For three hours Jesus hangs on the Cross after the soldiers nailed Him there. Jesus offers His death on the Cross for the salvation of the whole world. Mary is standing at the foot of the Cross. She suffers in soul with Jesus. Mary, too, offers the Sacrifice of her Son to God the Father. At holy Mass, like Mary, I, too, can offer Jesus. At every holy Sacrifice of the Mass, Jesus offers the same Sacrifice of the Cross, and I offer it, too.

The Glorious Mysteries
— Sundays and Wednesdays

1. The Resurrection of Our Lord: Jesus is risen. Having died on the Cross, Jesus lives again. Jesus appears to many people after He comes back to life. Jesus proves that He is really God by dying as Man and coming back to life in His real Body. The same risen Body of Jesus that is now in heaven becomes present at Mass in the Holy Eucharist. St. Mary Magdalene falls at the feet of Jesus to adore Him after He rises from the dead. I can both adore Jesus in the Blessed Sacrament and receive Him into my soul.

2. The Ascension of Our Lord: After forty days on earth since rising from the dead, Jesus returns to heaven. Jesus disappears into the clouds. The Apostles stand there and are filled with happiness that Mary is still with them. The Mother of the Church stays on earth to help the Apostles in their work. Jesus promises that, together with the Father, He will send them the Holy Spirit. The Apostles received the power to offer holy Mass and bring Jesus back to earth in the Holy Eucharist. How happy and full of love and adoration must Mary have been whenever one of the Apostles offered Mass. I ask Mary to lend me the faith and love of her Immaculate Heart to help participate in the holy Mass.

3. The Descent of the Holy Spirit: The Holy Spirit first came down upon Mary when God became Man. Now the Holy Spirit comes down upon the

Church. Both Mary and the disciples are set on fire with the Holy Spirit, who comes like a mighty wind. Tongues of fire settle down upon each of them. It is the birthday of the Church. The Mother of the Church, Mary, must be present when the Church is born. At every Sacrifice of the Mass, the Church is present in a special way. The Father is worshiped. Jesus is present. The power of the Holy Spirit acts again. Through the Holy Eucharist, Jesus makes us all one in Himself. Mary our Mother rejoices.

4. The Assumption of the Blessed Virgin: It was like heaven on earth whenever Mary was present at Mass after Jesus ascended into heaven. Finally, Jesus drew the body of His holy Mother to heaven. Jesus has promised that if we eat His Body and drink His Blood, He will raise us up. Mary is so full of love that she does not have to wait until the end of the world. By the holy Mass and by the Blessed Sacrament, we prepare to go to heaven in soul and finally in body.

5. The Coronation of Mary: All of the angels and saints and Jesus Himself receive Mary into heaven. The Blessed Trinity crowns her as Queen. As Queen and Mother, Mary still prays for us on earth. Through the Holy Eucharist, the Body of her Son (which Mary first gave us), the Blessed Mother still prays to draw us all into one in her Son.

Chaplet of Divine Mercy

This devotion is to be prayed using ordinary rosary beads.

Begin with the Our Father, Hail Mary, and Apostles' Creed. On the five large beads (Our Father beads), say the following:

Eternal Father, I offer You the Body and Blood, Soul and Divinity of Your dearly beloved Son, our Lord Jesus Christ, in atonement for our sins and those of the whole world.

On the ten small beads (Hail Mary beads), say the following:

For the sake of His sorrowful Passion, have mercy on us and on the whole world.

Conclude with the following (three times):

Holy God, Holy Mighty One, Holy Immortal One, have mercy on us and on the whole world.

(Imprimatur Curia Metropolitan, Kraków, February 16, 1980, ✠ Franciszek Macharski)

The Way of the Cross

Opening Prayer: My Jesus, may I walk in Your footprints as You make the Way of the Cross to Calvary. I want to put on Your mind. I want to relive with You, my Lord and my God, Your sufferings and Your sacrifice. Amen.

First Station: *Jesus is condemned to death.* Jesus, You are standing before Pontius Pilate to be judged. The crowds of people You have taught and loved have been turned against You. Pilate knows You are innocent. He is weak and gives in to the crowd. You are condemned to die on the Cross. O Jesus, when I am falsely accused I will think of You being judged guilty. You were not guilty of any sins Yourself. You took the guilt of my sins and those of the world upon Yourself. My Jesus, my sins, too, caused You to be condemned to death.

Second Station: *Jesus takes up His Cross.* Jesus, You accept the Cross to carry to Mt. Calvary because it is the will of Your Father. It is not easy to carry that heavy Cross. But You carry it because You love God and You love us. My Jesus, You said that unless we take up our cross daily and follow You, we are not worthy of You. Things are hard for me sometimes. There are things I don't like to do, things I find hard to accept. I will take them up as my cross and follow You, my Jesus.

Third Station: *Jesus falls the first time.* The Cross is so heavy, dear Jesus, that You fall to the ground. You love the world so much, but now its sins have crushed You to the ground. You look to the millions of souls You will save. You get up again and continue on. Jesus, sometimes I fall. Even though I try hard, I fail. I have sinned through my own fault more than once, Jesus. I am sorry. Thank You for making it possible for me to get up again and follow You.

Fourth Station: *Jesus meets His Blessed Mother.* O Jesus, You would rather that Your Blessed Mother Mary did not have to see You this way. People are cursing and making fun of You. You are bleeding and are covered with sweat and dust. Your sorrowful and Immaculate Mother looks at You with deepest faith and love. She wishes she could take up the Cross for You. Seeing the great faith and love of Your Mother renews Your strength. You continue on. My Jesus, when life seems difficult for me, I, too, will look to Your Mother, Mary. Her sorrowful and Immaculate Heart will give me strength to try harder to follow You.

Fifth Station: *Simon helps Jesus carry the Cross.* The soldiers notice how tired and weak You are becoming, Jesus. It is not because they feel sorry for You that they make Simon help You carry the Cross. They just want to make sure You make it to the top of the hill so You can be crucified. Simon does not want to help You. When he notices Your tender love and kindness, however, Simon more willingly helps

You. What a great grace it was for Simon to be able to help You carry the Cross. He did not know that at first. Just as I don't know at times that things that are hard for me are really good for my soul. I can offer them up in reparation for the conversion of sinners. Jesus, when I help others for love of You, it is the same as doing it to You.

Sixth Station: *Veronica wipes the face of Jesus.* Jesus, on Your way to be crucified, a woman named Veronica breaks through the crowd. She has noticed Your face bloody and dirty with sweat and dust. She feels so sorry for You. She takes a cloth and wipes Your face. Something of the goodness of Your Blessed Mother and of Yourself, dear Jesus, is reflected in this woman. Because of her kindness, You leave an image of Your holy face upon her cloth. O Jesus, place the image of Yourself upon my soul. If I do good things for You in others, You will imprint Your goodness, Your holiness upon me. O holy face of Jesus, look upon me. Have pity on me and upon all sinners in the whole world.

Seventh Station: *Jesus falls the second time.* How heavy the Cross falls upon You this time, dear Jesus. How You love everyone. But they are making fun of You, laughing at You, spitting at You. Jesus, You are feeling so much pain in Your Body. But You hurt even more in Your heart. I want to comfort You with my love. When people do wrong to me, dear Jesus, and make fun of me, I shall be brave for love of You. I shall get up and continue on, as You did.

Eighth Station: *Jesus speaks to the women and their children.* O how You love children, my Jesus. You often put Your arms around children and bless them. And now here You meet mothers and their children. How sad You are in soul to have them see You carrying Your Cross to Your death. Jesus, You do not want the women to feel sorry for You. You tell them to pray for themselves and their children. Even when You have so much to suffer, You try to comfort others. Jesus, help me remember to comfort others in need.

Ninth Station: *Jesus falls the third time.* My Jesus, will You ever be able to get up again? It is so hard for You to carry the Cross up the hill of Calvary. The soldiers are worried that You will not be able to make it to the top. But You get up again and struggle on. My Jesus, because You fell due to our sins, I tell myself that when I fall into sin, I can rise again by making a good confession.

Tenth Station: *Jesus is stripped of His garments.* Jesus, they pull off Your clothes, and the wounds of Your Body are opened again. You have to stand in front of people that way. The crowd seems to have no feelings for You, dear Jesus, You who only love souls. You do not complain. My Jesus, help me to do the right thing always. Even when others make fun, I shall still do what is right. I'll not complain when wrongs are done to me.

Eleventh Station: *Jesus is nailed to the Cross.* My Jesus, they pull Your feet and arms to the place prepared for the big nails. Then they drive the nails through Your Body. Oh, how terrible the pain is! The precious Blood from Your sacred Body flows again so as to redeem the world. Thank You, dear Jesus, for suffering so much for me and for the sins of everyone. Give me strength, dear Jesus, when I must suffer, and cannot go where I want, or do what I want, to offer it in union with Your sufferings. In this way, I can lessen Your sufferings.

Twelfth Station: *Jesus dies on the Cross.* For three long hours You hang on the Cross, my Jesus. Because You love souls and Your heavenly Father so much, You permit Yourself to be lifted up on the Cross. Your Blessed Mother stands beneath the Cross. A sword of sorrow has pierced through her sweet soul. The Immaculate Heart of Mary suffers together with You, Jesus. All the sins that wound Your Sacred Heart wound her heart as well. How sorrowful is Mary when You bow Your head and die. O Mary, you prayed on Calvary for the conversion of sinners. I join my prayers and sacrifices to yours so that souls will be saved. Lead the souls in purgatory to heaven soon.

Thirteenth Station: *Jesus is taken down from the Cross.* Jesus, when they take You down from the Cross, they place You in the sweet arms of Your Mother. Again, she offers Your great Sacrifice to the heavenly Father for the sins of the whole world. Sweet heart of Mary, through your prayers and offerings, be my salvation in Jesus Christ.

Fourteenth Station: *The Body of Jesus is laid in the tomb.* They wrap Your holy Body in linen cloths, dear Jesus. Then it is laid in a tomb cut out of a hill of rock. Your Blessed Mother stays with You to the last. The apostle John is still with her. The others run away in fear. My Jesus, I will always stay with You. Even when I am afraid, I will know that You are at my side. Your Blessed Mother will help me, too. The Body of Jesus lies in the tomb awaiting resurrection.

Closing Prayer: Thank You, Jesus, for permitting me to walk to Calvary with You again. I believe that Your Body is now present in the Holy Eucharist. I know by faith that You are present in the tabernacles of the Catholic Church. Jesus, You will remain with us until the end of the world. I believe that every holy Mass perpetuates the Sacrifice of the Cross. Thank You for rising from the dead and for being present now in the Blessed Sacrament so as to lead souls to heaven. Amen.

(At the conclusion of the Stations, offer some prayers for the intentions of our Holy Father, the Pope.)

II

BASICS OF THE FAITH

The Eight Beatitudes
(From Matthew 5:3-10)

- Blessed are the poor in spirit; the reign of God is theirs.
- Blessed are the sorrowing; they shall be consoled.
- Blessed are the lowly; they shall inherit the land.
- Blessed are they who hunger and thirst for holiness; they shall have their fill.
- Blessed are they who show mercy; mercy shall be theirs.
- Blessed are the single-hearted; they shall see God.
- Blessed are the peacemakers; they shall be called sons of God.
- Blessed are those persecuted for holiness' sake; the reign of God is theirs.

The Ten Commandments

1. I am the Lord your God. You shall not have strange gods before Me.
2. You shall not take the Name of the Lord your God in vain.
3. Remember to keep holy the Lord's Day.
4. Honor your father and your mother.
5. You shall not kill.
6. You shall not commit adultery.
7. You shall not steal.
8. You shall not bear false witness against your neighbor.

9. You shall not covet your neighbor's wife.
10. You shall not covet your neighbor's goods.

Jesus said: "You must love the Lord your God with all your heart, with all your soul, and with all your mind. This is the greatest and the first commandment. The second resembles it: You must love your neighbor as yourself. On these two commandments hang the whole law, and the prophets also" (Matthew 22:37-40).

Jesus also said: "If you love Me you will keep My commandments" (John 14:15).

The Seven Sacraments

The Sacraments were given to the Church by Jesus Christ.

Baptism: A rebirth as a child of God made holy by the Spirit. Gives the sharing of God's life; cleanses from original sin and personal sins; makes one a member of the community of the Church. The indelible seal of Jesus on the soul from baptism can never be erased. It joins us to Jesus as Priest, Prophet, and King.

Confirmation: Gives a special seal of the Holy Spirit. It gives us special spiritual strength to make Jesus known in the world and to live in the world as Christ would.

Penance: Gives us the merciful forgiveness of God through the priest when we confess our sins sincerely, in true sorrow and with the intention to avoid sin in the future. It gives the help of Jesus to over-come habits of sin and grow in perfection.

Holy Orders: Gives the special power of Jesus to priests. A special indelible seal of Jesus is given to the soul. It gives the priest the power to forgive sins in Jesus' Name, change bread and wine into the Body and Blood of Jesus, and perpetuate the Sacrifice of the Cross, which is the Mass. It also gives the power to anoint the sick. By this Sacrament, the Holy Spirit helps priests and bishops guide the Church and be shepherds to the faith community.

Anointing of the Sick: The Sacrament for the seriously ill, infirm, and aged. It sanctifies sufferings, increases grace, forgives sins, and makes one ready for heaven. It sometimes heals the body as well as the soul.

Holy Eucharist: The greatest of the Sacraments. It is both a *Sacrifice*, in the celebration of Mass, and a *Sacrament*, as present in the tabernacle and which we receive in Holy Communion. In the Mass, Jesus acts to offer the Sacrifice of the Cross. In the Blessed Sacrament, Jesus is present for us to adore, to receive.

Sacrament of Matrimony: The joining of hus-band and wife in Christ until death. It gives special graces to husband and wife and to parents and loyal spouses.

The Chief Corporal Works of Mercy

- To feed the hungry.
- To give drink to the thirsty.

- To clothe the naked.
- To visit the imprisoned.
- To shelter the homeless.
- To visit the sick.
- To bury the dead.

Jesus said, "As you did this to one of the least of these brothers of Mine, you did it to Me" (Matthew 25:40), and "If anyone gives you a cup of water to drink just because you belong to Christ, then I tell you solemnly, he will most certainly not lose his reward"(Mark 9:41).

The Chief Spiritual Works of Mercy
- To admonish the sinner.
- To instruct the ignorant.
- To counsel the doubtful.
- To comfort the sorrowful.
- To bear wrongs patiently.
- To forgive all injuries.
- To pray for the living and the dead.

The Seven Capital Sins
- **Pride:** Thinking too highly of one's own excellence.
- **Covetousness:** Wanting the things of this world too strongly.
- **Lust:** Wanting to give pleasure to one's body in a wrong way.
- **Anger:** Seeking revenge; losing one's temper.

- **Gluttony:** Eating or drinking too much.
- **Envy:** Sad when others have good things; being jealous.
- **Sloth:** Lazy in seeking spiritual things; not caring about the soul.

ICON OF OUR LADY OF SOUFANIEH

Special Duties of Catholics:
The Precepts of the Church

The list below is taken from the *Catechism of the Catholic Church* (2041-2043). This is the catechism for the Church, for the entire world, approved by Pope John Paul II.

1. "You shall attend Mass on Sundays and on holy days of obligation and rest from servile labor."
2. "You shall confess your sins at least once a year."
3. "You shall receive the sacrament of the Eucharist at least during the Easter season."
4. "You shall observe the days of fasting and abstinence established by the Church."
5. "You shall help to provide for the needs of the Church."
6. The faithful also have the duty of providing for the material needs of the Church, each according to his abilities.

The duties listed above consist of the minimum that is expected of a Catholic.